I'm Afraid He's Doing His Best

I'm Afraid He's Doing His Best

Fifty Years of Education

John and David Sidnell

Matador
5 Weir Road
Kibworth Beauchamp
Leicester LE8 0LQ, UK
Tel: (+44) 116 279 2299
Fax: (+44) 116 279 2277
Email: books@troubador.co.uk
Web: www.troubador.co.uk/matador

ISBN 978 1848765 726

British Library Cataloguing in Publication Data.
A catalogue record for this book is available from the British Library.

Typeset in 12pt Palatino by Troubador Publishing Ltd, Leicester, UK

Matador is an imprint of Troubador Publishing Ltd

Printed in Great Britain by the MPG Books Group, Bodmin and King's Lynn

INTRODUCTION

Schools have changed out of all recognition over the last fifty years. Here, John and David Sidnell recollect teaching long before the days of Health and Safety, first as teachers and later as Headmasters. A flavour of the contents can be judged by their opening remarks often made to new parents, 'If you promise not to believe everything that you may hear goes on in school, I'll promise not to believe what your offspring tell us that goes on at home!'

David and John Sidnell are identical twins born in September 1928. The book traces their lives in pre- war London, through war time days, their time conscripted in the army and finally, their near identical teaching careers, both retiring as Headmasters. Sharing so many life experiences, they have remained close throughout their lives.

The birth was a great surprise to their mother who was told, even on the day, that she was expecting just a bonny boy. They were inseparable from the moment they were born and that close bond lasted all their lives.

David tended to be more intelligent, but relied heavily upon John's greater strength to get him out of problems with bigger boys at school. Their education was undoubtedly affected by moving out of London just before the war and joining a junior school in St. Albans that boasted of a scholarship system that largely depended on the status and income of the parents. The boys were sent to a very new secondary school with excellent facilities, but almost immediately a school evacuated from London joined them making the building very overcrowded. The young enthusiastic masters were conscripted into the forces and their places taken by inexperienced lady teachers. As all pupils left at fourteen and a very great deal of time was spent playing cards in the air raid shelters or helping with the war effort, it was not surprising the boys knew very little when they left.

It was due to the tireless efforts of their father, that they were coached intensively until they were conscripted into the army at eighteen. Their efforts to improve themselves continued when they were accepted on a course to Göttingen University, for teacher training and on leaving the army were accepted into Westminster College where they gained the college prize for teaching.

Before this book was completed David sadly died. I should like to dedicate this book to him for his enthusiasm in starting this project and his great sense of humour, which, I'm sure will amuse readers.

John Sidnell

ACKNOWLEDGEMENTS

My sincere thanks to Andre Hess for his guidance and advice in the preparation of this book and without whose help its production would not have been possible.

FOREWORD

The first time John and David were at Beaumont School was as pupils at the age of eleven. However, they returned in their 70's to speak to 13 and 14 year old pupils who are now known as Year Nine.

As a teacher with 16 years experience, I still find this group of children most challenging to engage. There are a plethora of reasons for this, raging hormones being the most prevalent!

I must admit on our first meeting John and David, although they were immensely polite, charming and erudite, with years of experience of teaching primary children, I had my doubts that this would sufficiently equip them to cope with our hundred potentially truculent teenagers! I'm delighted to be able to say I could not have been more wrong! From the moment John and David began to speak I could see "the lights go on" in our pupils' eyes, minds and hearts. The way the twins spoke, engaged but did not patronize. Their personal anecdotes and reflections brought their memories alive. Pupils responded with enthusiasm and sensitivity; they had lots of questions.

After their talk I was astounded to see some pupils had forgone their lunchtime to stay behind as they wanted to speak to John and David personally. I knew at that point we would be inviting them back to speak next year…..

John and David returned several times annually. Year 9, having heard from their older peers, would ask 'When are the old Beaumont people coming in?' After each visit pupils send cards and letters to show their appreciation.

After David's death, John returned alone, determined to maintain what has become an integral part of the History curriculum. My favourite pupil quote written after John's first solo visit was "Sidnell, you are a legend". This equally applies to David.

On both a personal and professional level I am delighted that so many Beaumont pupils, both past and present have had the pleasure of hearing John and David. They are truly inspiring and great teachers.

(Ms) Leigh Wensley BA (Hons) MA. PGCE
History Teacher Beaumont School

CHAPTER 1

What Have You Got For A Penny?

We lived in a terraced house identical in most respects to dozens of others in Putney before the war. Our father planted two poplar trees at the bottom of our very small garden, naming one John and the other one David. Several times a week a little old man appeared down the road, pulling a heavy wooden cart covered with a canvas hood, not unlike a miniature version of the wagons driven by the early American settlers. He was bent nearly in half pulling the heavy load and his face, exposed to all weathers, was like wrinkled leather. When he straightened his back to call his wares, he always had a smile for his customers. It was only by looking carefully in his cart that the meaning of his cries became clear. In that jumble of sound, he let the world know that he was selling vinegar, paraffin, starch crystals, dolly blue, gas mantels, pot menders, lamp wicks, fountain pen ink, the list was endless.

If we had been good we were allowed to spend our 'Saturday penny' at Whites Bazaar, a short distance from home. A gentleman, who was undoubtedly the most patient man in the world, owned it. His shop was a wonderland of cheap, foreign toys. His heart must have sunk when we appeared with monotonous regularity with the request "What have you got for a penny?" With endless patience and good humour, he arranged a line of toys on the counter; a lead soldier, a wooden top, a small cannon that fired match sticks, ten marbles in a cotton bag and perhaps the most tantalising, a small steel bomb! The 'bomb' was discouraged by our parents after we discovered that a roll of caps could be cut up and the chamber primed with at least a dozen. The resulting loud explosion frequently brought neighbours to their doors. It was fortunate that our father did not discover our skill at making lethal weapons. It was not long before we devised a cannon made out of a short length of copper tubing blocked at one end. We carefully sharpened the end of a six-inch nail as the projectile and cut open a box of caps to act as the explosive. The weapon was held in a simple wooden cradle and fired by placing a candle under the barrel containing the explosive. Our first experiment was nearly the last, as we lit the candle and hid behind a clump of trees some twenty yards away. We had nearly given up hope of the gun working when there was a loud explosion and we found the sharpened nail head buried in the tree a few feet from where we were standing. Perhaps it was fortunate that the force of the explosion destroyed our cannon!

The one concession to modern life in the 30's was a large Marconi wireless set powered by a heavy glass accumulator. Most of the houses in our area had no electricity. With sparing use the accumulator would last a week. It was then taken to the local hardware store to be recharged for sixpence. Through the background of whistles and crackles, we listened to the Children's Hour with Uncle Mac, David and Auntie Violet. We loved Toy Town, with Mr Grouser,

Mr Mayor and Larry the Lamb. Later, the BBC did a wonderful series entitled 'Castles of England' by L. Du Garde Peach. This pre war radio began our love of history.

Our Grandfather, who lived only a few minutes walk away, had a wonderful fund of stories to tell of his life starting from 1867. He began as an apprentice to a wheelwright, living in the village of Manuden on the Hertfordshire – Essex border. His day began with a two-hour session in the sawpit. He kept us enthralled by his descriptions of the various woods used and the skill needed to make a carriage wheel. At 21, however, he made his way to London, where he found a job at Spinks, the Piccadilly Jewellers. There he spent the rest of his working life as the doorman, greeting the rich and famous from the four corners of the world. Sometimes the police in a hansom cab would pick him up in the early hours if burglars were thought to be on the premises. The police always insisted he went in first, as 'He knew the way!' Granddad distrusted this suggestion, as he was sure that if he disturbed the burglars, he would get the first bullet!

Perhaps the most memorable story relating to Grandfather's time at Spinks, was the occasion when a large group of foreign dignitaries were examining some very expensive Japanese vases. Without warning one toppled off its stand and smashed to pieces on the floor. Granddad begged for the broken pieces and painstakingly stuck them all together with a tube of glue. That vase was the subject of a BBC Sunday morning TV broadcast given by me in 1985. Working in the centre of London, Granddad attended Queen Victoria's Diamond Jubilee and a few years later joined the crowds with heads bowed at her funeral. Granddad died at 92. He was a tall, active man walking at least a mile every day until a few months before his death. In later life he bore a striking resemblance to Sir Edward Elgar.

George Moss – Grandfather to John and David.

CHAPTER 2

Early School Days In London 1934 – 1938

WEST HILL PUTNEY, Our Primary School

We had many childhood illnesses in pre war days and we were six before we finally joined West Hill School Putney. The girls were accommodated on the top floor and the boys on the second floor. The iron letters on the school gates announced 'Mixed Infants' on the ground floor. Our first teacher was Miss Pinney. She was a pleasant lady, but the Headmistress, Miss Kipps, could have figured in a Dickens novel. She wore pince-nez glasses on the end of her nose and had her lips pressed tightly together at all times.

There was unnecessary control over children's

behaviour in the classroom. Whenever the Headmistress came into the classroom we had to put down our pencils or slates and stand quietly, awaiting the order from Miss Kipps to sit. No talking was allowed and certainly no fidgeting. Not until the monitor had closed the door on the Headmistress were we allowed to relax. As young as we were, I had the feeling that the teacher was as nervous of Miss Kipps as we were! Looking back over seventy years that was never the sort of respect I wanted from any children in my school. In her place I should have asked to see their work and given praise where possible.

An Infants classroom at West Hill School. David and John are sitting at the back table on the right .circa .1934

We were taught the three R's for most of the day. Our reading was assisted and encouraged by large posters displayed on the brown glazed brick walls. Neither of us had any difficulty in learning to read. The fact that we kept these reading books for years after leaving the school indicates how much we treasured them.

Physical training was held in the playground, where we stood in straight lines at the command of Miss Pinney's whistle. Once a week we lined up with our spoons to receive a dose of cod liver oil and malt. I can still recall the vile taste to this day. We must have been sickly children, as the doctor suggested a weekly treatment of ultra violet light. For this we sat in our underwear around an intense light wearing dark glasses. We only later understood that this was the accepted treatment and prevention of Rickets.

We particularly remember Empire Day. The whole school marched round the playground, with the Head Boy proudly holding the Union Jack. The Head master opened his window on the ground floor and positioned his gramophone with it's huge horn to amplify the sound, playing 'Land of Hope and Glory'. At the end of the march we retired to the main hall where we received a cup of lemonade.

We moved to St Albans in 1938. Dad had been working in a shipping office in London, but he lost his job like so many others at that time. We knew little about his work except that he was able to bring home postage stamps from all over the world. In later years these proved to be very valuable. My mother's uncle offered Dad a job behind the counter in a tool shop in St Albans at a very low weekly wage. He also offered dad £700 as a loan to buy a bungalow on a new estate. How Dad managed to pay ten shillings a week out of his wage of £4 10/-, I shall never know. It was some years later that Dad realised the loan was advanced with the hope that John and I would follow him and work behind the counter, but he had very different plans for our future.

On one occasion in our school holidays, we were asked to paint rusting ammunition boxes that could be later sold as tool boxes .For a day's work we were paid half a crown [12 ½ p each]. We painted fifteen boxes in about eight hours! That money meant so much to us. We spent hours deciding how we should spend it. Our parents were good in allowing us to go on 'adventures' on a Saturday, provided we always kept together. We loved to spend our pocket money, catching a train and exploring nearby towns. Just before Christmas, we made a 'special' journey to Hendon, which seemed to us to be on the edge of the world!

We visited Woolworths and bought mum her Christmas present. It was a tiny bottle of 'Ashes of Roses' for 1/6p. Mum was always delighted, but in retrospect, I can't imagine what scent costing one shilling and six pence must have really smelt like!

The family loved living in this vast orchard, which was being developed into a housing estate. Our bungalow was surrounded by fruit trees. Consequently we were able to bring sacks full of apples, pears and plums for mum to bottle in Kilner jars. Such jars were very popular before and during the war. They were made of thick clear glass with a seal also made of glass. There were occasions when we arrived on the doorstep with sack full of fruit, that mum would wipe her hand across her forehead and say 'Not more. Surely not more boys!'

Perhaps we should draw a veil over the less sensible activities enjoyed during that period of our lives. But we cannot do that without mentioning the races we had across the top rafters of half built houses; the lighting of bundles of fireworks, throwing them down half built sewers, and the amplified noise putting birds to flight all over the estate.

We also recall fondly and most memorably, making a go cart and soaking the rear curtained seating compartment with paraffin and setting it ablaze, launching it down a steep hill to the woods at the bottom. I can only think that we must have been reading about Viking funerals at the time!

CHAPTER 3

Alma Road School St Albans – Caught In a Time Warp

Alma Road School St Albans

We attended the local primary school and from its grim appearance, obviously untouched since it was built in Victorian times. It boasted of two playgrounds. A small one for the juniors was made even smaller by a plantation of diseased laurel bushes running the length of one side. Any attempt to retrieve a ball from this forbidden area merited one stroke of the cane. The playground designated for the infants was even smaller. The interior of the building was typically Victorian, dark lit with gas lamps and tall, narrow windows invariably stuck open or shut. The tiered classroom accommodated over twenty, double desks of unsuitable design. They had a narrow oak plank as a seat and the ledge under the desks tops was so narrow that exercise books continually clattered to the floor. The desks were deeply carved with the initials of children who, in later years, became respected citizens of the town. Each desk had two inkwells filled by a lucky monitor every Friday. As the china inkwells were never cleaned, one learned not to dip too deeply for fear of dragging up accumulated dirt from the last fifty years. Much of our time was devoted to developing a good style of cursive handwriting, learning our times table by rote, writing short stories and learning poems. Many of these we can still recite to this day. The headmistress had little time for children from working class families, particularly slow learners. When Dad enquired if she thought we would benefit from Grammar School education, he was told in no uncertain terms that the few places available would go to children from professional classes!

As Dad worked behind the counter in a tool shop, convention meant that we were placed at a secondary modern school opened two years previously.

Beaumont School St Albans –
Child Labour in the Wartime

Beaumont School Buildings St Albans.

Beaumont was built in 1938 to accommodate girls upstairs and, very strictly segregated, boys downstairs. There was never any attempt to allow the boys and girls to mix under any circumstances. We might just as well have been in buildings a mile apart! Any boy daring to look up at the upstairs windows was either caned or sent upstairs to share the rest of the day in a classroom full of girls! Most boys preferred the cane! Readers may be interested to hear that I dared the school punishment and waved to a pretty girl when we first arrived at the school. Years later, she became my wife and we were happily married for over fifty years.

The school was, nevertheless, beautifully equipped with a gymnasium, showers, superbly equipped rooms for art, science and geography. It also boasted separate woodwork and metalwork centres. We were told of all the things we could make, depending on our skills, from simple lamp brackets to bedroom stools and even a chest of drawers using secret mitred dovetails. Everything stretched ahead as a wonderful dream, but within a few months the War started and our dreams turned to ashes, as all available rooms were occupied by evacuees from a London school. We hated them, failing to appreciate that many were bombed out and all were far from home. To add to our miseries, most of our enthusiastic young masters left to join the forces and were replaced by elderly teachers, reluctantly persuaded from retirement and supported, if that is the right word, by young lady teachers who had completed just thirteen months emergency training.

Quite understandably, the latter faced problems never envisaged in their worst nightmares, when confronted by forty resentful, rebellious boys. The elderly masters used the cane on any and every occasion. The following story will illustrate.

Several classes of boys were lined up across the playground. Very few had any idea why they were there standing in the cold. Finally, one boy was barged forward by the master. "This is the boy who is going to get the caning of his life", he shouted and struck the boy hard across the seat of his trousers with his cane. We watched as the master brought the cane down with great force on the boy's outstretched hands. The boy was not one of our friends, but no one deserved to be caned so harshly. The master continued, "Now go to the Headmaster and tell him, you deserved to be caned for being a liar and a thief". We all felt sorry for him, especially as we heard that he received two more strokes on his backside from the Head. My brother and I collected our cycles from the cycle shed and there, standing beside his cycle, was the boy who had been so severely punished. He simply said,

"Can I borrow yer 'andkerchiefs Sidnells please?" This boy never said 'Please' for anything, but both hands were bleeding from the caning and he couldn't hold the handlebars properly. We wrapped the handkerchiefs round his bleeding fingers and helped him on the saddle because he was in so much pain. We rode on either side of him, pushing him the two miles to the council estate where he lived. When we told Dad about the incident, he simply said, "That master will be in trouble!" The following morning we went to school early to meet the boy who had been so badly treated. He had managed to cycle to school but his hands were badly cut and bruised "I don't fink I can 'old a pen Sid", he said. I brushed aside the remark, "But what did your father say?" I asked, expecting at the very least a confrontation between the Head and the parent. "Nuffink" he answered. "He said, It served me right". So what was his crime that had disrupted the school for the best part of an afternoon? He had picked up a birds egg!

In those early wartime days we had no option but to devote much of our time to helping with the war effort. Hence, nearly all the usual lessons were replaced by making hospital screens, repairing ammunition boxes, and rough filing machine gun sights. We were also taken down to Oaklands for every sort of farm work including potato-planting, and picking and during the summer holidays we were told it was our duty to help with the harvest. The jobs were endless. We were paid a few pence an hour to begin with, but later we were given four Horlicks tablets instead for two hours work! We learned many years later that boys working for the war effort under the age of fourteen should have their parents written consent. This was never mentioned at the time by the Headmaster. He was, however, the best teacher in the department. There was always a great sense of anticipation when he announced 'Its *History* this afternoon boys!' On one occasion he produced a diary from a serving officer in the Peninsula War, pleading for new boots for his men who had completely worn through those they were wearing. We really looked forward to his lessons, but they were few and far between.

We had the occasional science lesson and I remember trying to amaze our science teacher by making a small model aircraft, which we suspended on a wire. On being pulled over the target, we switched off the battery and an iron bomb dropped on the target below. We explained that this demonstrated electromagnetism. He made absolutely no comment and didn't even glance over to our experiment but continued to cover the blackboard with his thin spidery writing about experiments we had not actually seen.

We were wasting our time!

For a few months we enjoyed art lessons, but all too soon the Art teacher joined the Air Force. As clearly as David remembers those excellent history lessons given by the Headmaster, I must confess to remembering a far less pleasant experience that happened to me. As my brother mentioned earlier, I had been very interested in pen and ink drawings and very much enjoyed art generally. On one grey afternoon in the spring term our lady teacher, obviously hoping to keep the boys quiet at any cost said "I want all you boys to draw something you are interested in and I will say which one I think is the best." We spent an hour producing our pictures and I have to say I was well pleased with my effort. I explained to the teacher it was meant to represent the

Battle of Bosworth Field in 1485 between Henry VII and King Richard III. She liked it and announced she would take it home and frame it. I was absolutely delighted and even the other boys in the class congratulated me. After all, success did not often come my way! I left school, elated with the news and then I remembered I had left my homework book in my desk and returned to the classroom to collect it. The class teacher was leaving as I entered the classroom. I explained I had left my homework book in my desk. She smiled briefly and hurried off. I collected my book and as I left the classroom, I noticed a pile of paper in the waste bin. I hesitated and turned over the top sheet of paper. It was my picture torn in two, together with all the other pictures we had spent an hour producing! I was completely bewildered. How could she say such nice things about my picture and then tear it up? The fact I can still remember the incident over seventy years later proves what a damaging impression it made on me!

Unfortunately, so much of the time was wasted by finding an answer to such questions as £1972 .19s. 7¾d x127! Even in those far off days, I failed to see their relevance in every day life. My father earned £4-10/- a week and numbers in the thousands were quite outside our understanding.

Occasionally the war came a little too close. We arrived at school one morning to find several craters in the school field. The Headmaster said he knew of no moles that could dig holes that deep and we were sent home for the day while a number of unexploded bombs were removed. Soon, air raid shelters were provided. They were unheated, damp and lacking in proper toilet facilities. When the siren sounded, we filed down to the shelters to sit on hard wooden benches, sometimes for hours at a time. The masters stood at the entrances and smoked cigarettes, allowing us to play cards. We heard the girls continued with their normal lessons in the shelters. In retrospect, the girls gained a huge advantage. The teachers from the boy's school simply weren't interested. Incidentally, at the tender age of twelve, I realised what a waste of time playing cards was and I never played another game in all my life.

On another occasion, a neat hole was found to be the site of an unexploded anti aircraft shell. Further interruption was caused when a large unexploded German bomb was to be detonated next to a water tower some half a mile from the school. The entire school and staff lined up round the perimeter fence for the deadline at 11.00am. We all hoped the huge concrete water tower would be blown to smithereens at the very least. On the appointed hour there was a loud explosion and a great mass of sandbags and dirt were thrown into the sky, but the tower stood as firm as a rock. Needless to say the boys were very disappointed! Finally, on one foggy November morning, we heard a low flying aircraft. Several of us predicted that it was not the sound of an English aeroplane. How right we were! Minutes later there was a very loud explosion, which rattled the windows, followed by a glow of fire in the direction of Hatfield aerodrome. We heard later that a German bomber had been disabled, but was able to drop a bomb through the open doors of the aerodrome some 2 miles away.

Prior to the war, school children swapped marbles and cigarette cards. In the early war time days, however, we swapped pieces of bombs, and parachute cord. The Germans frequently dropped air mines by parachute, the delayed action allowed the pilots more time to fly out of harm's way. We were told that mothers used the parachute silk to make underwear! Lastly, we clearly remember running across the school field in a snowstorm to see a giant barrage balloon. It had come adrift over London and came to rest when the cable became entangled round our goalposts!

It was not surprising we left Beaumont School at 13 ½ knowing little more than we did when we arrived. No effort was made to help us find employment and most boys did odd jobs or helped their fathers. The relative who employed Dad assumed that we would also serve behind the counter in his tool shop. By sheer chance, however, Dad found out that two free places were awarded annually at the local art school. We always enjoyed drawing in our spare time and sat the entrance examination. We were awarded the free places. For the next two years we were studying drawing, still life, architecture, memory drawing and colour combinations. We thoroughly enjoyed every minute of the course and much to the Principal's amusement, we asked if we could work away from the girls, as we found them distracting! John produced some commendable pen and inks and I still treasure a few watercolours painted 65 years ago.

Beaumont School by air (copyright)

CHAPTER FOUR

Edwin Robertson – Real Education Begins

Our Tutor Edwin Robertson

By great good fortune at the time we left the art school, a new minister came to our church. He had some outstanding qualities. He was the most patient teacher I have ever had the privilege of knowing. Our father asked him to tutor us, and he agreed. For two golden years we cycled to his house five mornings a week, three hours a morning. His enthusiasm was infectious and his teaching inspired. He introduced us to the worlds of poetry, literature, chemistry, maths, French and English. We read endlessly for pleasure. He took us to see Shakespeare's 'Macbeth' with Donald Woolfit, leading actor of the day, renowned for his Shakespearian roles. He conducted experiments in chemistry on his wife's kitchen table and for the first time in our lives we enjoyed being taught. Having never experienced real education before, we found everything very strange and quite difficult. We had just one thing in our favour: we both had excellent memories and whatever we heard, we remembered. David at this time caught a form of Poliomyelitis that left him paralysed for several months. It was very worrying for all concerned, but it offered unlimited reading time. His reading spanned novels by H. G. Wells, and even 'The Rise of the Dutch Republic' and 'The Rise and Fall of the Roman Empire'. It was hardly bedtime reading, but most enjoyable. One subject, however, always caused us difficulties. It was Algebra. Mr Robertson would set dozens of questions for us to attempt before the next week's lesson. I am ashamed to say we obliterated the fountain pen ticks with household bleach. On the following week he would re-tick the questions, only to find the ticks fading before his eyes on the bleach soaked paper! It is still a mystery to us both how Dad managed to pay Mr Robertson for all his hours of teaching. I do believe our father was an extremely handy man and I recall my mother doing the ironing for the Robertson family for many years, so I suppose some tuition was paid in kind. We attempted the London Matriculation examination and surprisingly passed in a credible number of subjects, but alas, not Mathematics. One can hardly be expected to cover the whole subject of mathematics to Matriculation standard from scratch in just two years. We are certainly not offering the following as an excuse for failure, but during the examination at London University, a V2 rocket landed nearby, bringing down dirt and dust. We were allowed ten minutes extra to complete the paper. In later life we became firm friends with Edwin, meeting him when we were in Germany just after the war. He became internationally known for his work with the German Protestant Churches and wrote nearly 100 books on religious topics over a period of some fifty years. He was truly a remarkable man. Indeed, he was inspirational.

We were fortunate to meet Mr Robertson again when we were conscripted into the army and posted to Germany just after the end of the war. We unexpectedly received a 'phone call from him, asking if it were possible to meet him in Hannover. This was very fortunate as we were stationed in the nearby town of Osnabrück. He announced he had been made Deputy Director of Religious Broadcasting and responsible for reorganisation of German churches. We were supplied with a jeep and driver and we literally had to pick our way through the bombed streets and mountains of rubble piled high, barely allowing sufficient room for the jeep to move forward. German civilians, dressed in rags picked their way through the rubble, their faces expressionless, staring at nothing with hollow eyes. We alighted and made our way to where we had been told the studio was situated. Then I became aware of a shabbily dressed woman holding the hands of two small children. She did not look up, but let the children creep forward. My knowledge of German was slight, but it did not need words to understand what the children wanted. They held their grubby hands forward for us to put something in them, their blue eyes, pleading more beseechingly than words ever could. Risking the non-fraternisation rule I reached into my greatcoat pocket and clutched a handful of wrapped sweets. The children's eyes lit up and I imagine for the first time in, perhaps months, a smile hovered around the mouth of this half-starved child. Even the mother bowed her head as a form of thanks. Soon we reached the house, which had been roughly converted into a very makeshift studio. Edwin acknowledged us through a glass screen, but almost immediately began this broadcast. I don't know what I expected, but the fact he was speaking in German came as a surprise. A few moments later the producer of the broadcast silently slid into the seat next to mine. He leaned towards me and I expected him to speak in German, which, to say the least was a cause of some concern as my German was rudimentary, but in perfect English he whispered, "Herr Robertson's German is much better than mine". After the broadcast was over, Edwin came through with the words," Come on boys, let's have a cup of tea." We remained friends with this remarkable man until he died quite recently in his mid nineties. Besides his writings, he had a keen interest in cricket and was a connoisseur of Italian wine.

CHAPTER 5

The Army – It Pays to Speak Up!

Like most young men we were conscripted into the army soon after the end of the War and were drafted to West Germany. After basic training, the memories of which still haunt me, we were posted to Larkhill, a camp on the Salisbury plains. We applied for a course on survey work where we received instruction on the use of the theodolite and range finders. We slept in a Nissan hut. This was in 1947 and it is on record that this was the coldest winter for almost a century. Most men taking courses were sent home on leave, but for reasons that no one ever bothered to explain, we were not! The huts were without any form of insulation and the tiny oyster stove situated at one end of the hut hardly created enough heat to warm the man lucky enough to be nearest to the fire!

It was not unusual to wake to find a layer of frost on beds further down the hut! Shaving was difficult since all water in the pipes was frozen solid and the warm water for shaving begged from the cookhouse was always cold by the time we reached the washroom.

Just one incident remains in my memory from that period before we were sent to Germany. The officers decided that the 25 pound guns should fire on a line of old German tanks which had been shipped over from Germany. Several of us were of the opinion that the young captain had not performed the exercise before!

Finally he came over to David and I to recheck the range of the tanks. The more I saw of his actions, the less convinced I was he knew what he was doing. Dave and I were becoming even more anxious, as readers may not be aware that the range finders position is considerably nearer the target than the guns! I whispered quietly to Dave when the officer retreated back to his command post that we were not going to be the object of some ghastly mistake and find 25 pound shells dropping short of their target and on the range finding position! I therefore calculated the range to be five hundred yards further than it actually was. The moment of firing approached and we peered anxiously through the lens of the range finder. A moment later we heard the sound of the guns firing and accordingly pressed our bodies hard into the bottom of a shallow trench we had dug. As soon as we heard the explosions we anxiously peered at the tanks. They were completely untouched, the shells landing, as we judged, some hundreds of yards beyond the target. More disturbingly they all landed to the right of the target! I gripped Dave's arm and pointed to a tree nearby. I hadn't taken account of the wind blowing quite strongly across the target. The officer called us 'incompetent fools', but we were of the opinion he should have, had he known how, checked our calculations. We heard nothing more of the incident and were drafted shortly afterwards to Germany and any records appeared to be 'lost in transit'.

It was a particularly cold night on Lüneburg Heath in Northern Germany, when we discovered we were guarding a hut containing an empty petrol can, an idea we had was to change our lives. We decided to ask the adjutant if we could give lectures on Current Affairs to the regiment. Amazingly, he agreed and sent us for a course at Göttingen University on Teaching Techniques. We loved every minute of it and were determined to become teachers. The adjutant decided to prove the course had been worthwhile by insisting we should jointly have to give an hour's lecture to the regiment. This was managed and we believed we heard some minute applause when we concluded! We were greatly encouraged! Unfortunately, within months, our regiment, 5th Royal Horse Artillery, was posted back to England. Even more seriously, it was decided by the Commanding Officer (C.O.) that there was no longer a need for an Education Department. This prompted the long serving Non-Commissioned Officers to use the men from education for tasks which weren't possible abroad under more enlightened officers. One of my first jobs was to white wash coal, which was used to edge the path to the officer's mess. Soon it became a serious pastime to apply for demobilisation courses before the NCO could think of any more stupid tasks for us to accomplish. When our demobilisation date was announced, we put up a chart and chalked off the days, much to the annoyance of the sergeant who had foolishly signed on for five years. Fortunately, the adjutant knew something of our work in Germany and when I requested a testimonial for us, he willingly agreed and was very fulsome in his praise of our achievements. Thus we completed our two years conscription and happily left that phase of our lives behind us.

Now ahead lay the task of convincing the authorities that we should be allowed to commence a course in teaching; something on which we had set our hearts, since our lessons with the troops after leaving Göttingen University.

CHAPTER 6

Into The Lion's Den.

We visited Westminster College in London with our father to seek a place for the Autumn Term. The Principal, J.S Ross, a cheery Scot, gave us the best possible advice in suggesting that we taught in local schools as unqualified teachers for the year prior to college. He rightly pointed out that we had no serious academic qualifications, not even a scholarship, but, depending on excellent, rather than good reports, he would 'take a chance' on us for the following year. His words were, "Don't let me down boys. This is the biggest gamble I have taken in twenty years." In retrospect, if the Principal had not taken that chance with us, we should have spent the rest of our lives serving behind a counter, following our father. We never thanked him enough for making such a financial sacrifice in allowing us to attend college, when our financial contribution would have obviously made such a difference to the standard of life for my parents. Over the years and particularly since the death of my father, I have pondered over this sad omission. Even to this day I can think of no satisfactory excuse. My father was a poor man who worked hard for little financial reward. He was not well educated in the accepted sense of the word. He was one of sixteen children, of whom two were brothers, one ten years older than he was and the other, many years younger.

When he came home from school, his task was to 'turn the mangle' for his mother, as his thirteen sisters all needed a clean petticoat and a clean dress every day. His father was nowhere to be seen in the evenings! Dad's father died before he reached fifty and his elder brother left home soon afterwards, leaving our father with even greater responsibilities towards the family. In later years he was always regarded as a' wise man' and later, when he asked Edwin Robertson to tutor David and I, my father was still referred to as "My wise councillor".

We were never conscious of having to "go without" as children. We were perhaps very fortunate in being brought up to accept gratefully what was given to us and never to expect more. There was just one occasion, as children when 'all the rules were broken' and David and I had the surprise of our lives. Our uncle Reg, whose profession had to do with the import of leather, lived in a fine house in Tooting. He had three sons and I recall that when we were about seven, he called to see us just before Christmas and brought round a box to be shared 'between us' for Christmas. On that extraordinary Christmas morning we saved his present until last. With trembling fingers we carefully unwrapped the coloured Christmas paper to reveal a cardboard box. We both knew what it contained! It was a magnificent Hornby clock engine and tender. Not in our wildest dreams did we expect such a present. Our father was equally surprised and told us after Christmas the engine would have cost uncle 27/6d and admitted he could never have afforded such an expensive gift. I am sure my brother would agree that our engine was undoubtedly the most surprising Christmas present we ever received.

CHAPTER 7

So This Was Teaching! – David Dips his Toe. September 1948.

Fleetville School entrance

I went to Fleetville School in St Albans under the Headship of Mr East. He was one of the very 'old school' and about to retire. I was given a class of 48 ten and eleven year olds. The 'classroom' was, in fact, a screened area in the hall right outside the Head's room, his door being left open except when he was on the phone. A constant stream of visitors to his room passed alongside my inadequately screened 'classroom', causing dozens of distractions, much to the delight of my children peering through cracks in the screen. Further problems were caused by a running commentary from an unseen, but clearly audible Headmaster. Me: "How many pounds are there in a stone, David Curran?" Seconds later the silence would be broken by an irritable voice from within. "Think boy, think! Mr Sidnell told you that only yesterday!" Mr East always assumed that any child waiting outside his room had been sent for punishment. The Friday register monitor accordingly viewed his job with considerable misgivings!

The morning assemblies were always the same meaningless ritual, starting with the entry music, thumped out on the piano by a well-meaning lady of indifferent musical ability. We sang the same hymn each day of the week, beginning with "Fight the good fight". The Head garbled two or three prayers at such speed that they sounded like a foreign language. The Lords Prayer was often finished in a single breath, "For Thine is the Kingdom, the Power and the Glory for ever and ever Amen. Lead on. No talking!" I have known him to answer the telephone in the middle of a prayer while the school waited with heads bowed for him to return and say "Amen". On another occasion I saw him shoulder his way through 'praying children' to clout a boy on the head at the back of the hall, who had been foolish enough to open his eyes. This was hardly a shining example of how to start the day in a reverent and thoughtful manner. My lowly position on the staff was soon made apparent to all. Within a few days of my arrival a large framed inscription appeared under the school clock in the Hall. It was written in script by the deputy head "Staff of Fleetville School 1948". There followed the names and qualifications of the staff in red ink, under which a line had been drawn. At the bottom of the inscription my name had been written in black ink with the word 'uncertified' beneath it. I think it should have read 'un-certificated' or perhaps 'certifiable'!

Although Fleetville School gave me the opportunity to teach children of all ages, it also gave me an insight into the workings of the old 11 + system. For this the children had to sit written papers in English, Arithmetic and an Intelligence Test. In reality the selection had begun years earlier when the children were segregated into A & B forms at the tender age of seven, the infant Head supplying a list of likely 'A' children. Under that system it could be argued that a child's path to University was predestined at the tender age of five! In the final year of the junior school children in the 'A' forms were given previous scholarship papers and coached in the best way to draft the answers. The 'B' forms were given no such advantage. To complete the charade, when the inevitable results were announced, the teacher would say, "Stand on your chairs those who have passed to Grammar Schools. You are the cream of St Albans and once again it proves what hard work will achieve". It is not difficult to envisage how such words went down with those who were not designated the 'cream'. The atmosphere in the staff room was not improved when the same teacher announced, "They came to me knowing nothing!"

There was certainly a contrast with the style of teaching and idiosyncrasies of the staff. There was a maiden lady nearly at retirement age, who always had the same mug for her tea at break times. A scene could be guaranteed if the mug was mistakenly given to a visitor. Then there was the only young lady on the staff, who never stayed behind after school for anything. At 3.45 pm she would open the classroom door, ahead of the children, reach up, and ring the home time bell and without breaking step, disappear through the double doors, homeward bound. Another male teacher, trusted with the formative education of the 3B, would shout to a naughty boy at the far end of the hall " 'ere, 'ere, 'ere, wot d'yur fink yer doing of? Get 'ere double quick." It soon became clear that I was resented by an elderly teacher whose class I took for English on Thursday afternoons. My main sin in her eyes was that I allowed the children to laugh and an even worse crime, I was young! On one occasion I was suggesting suitable endings for letters and in the speed of the moment I wrote 'sincerely' without the final 'e'. Once spotted, her reaction was as follows. "Stop children and put your pens down. Mr Sidnell has a confession to make! Come along, Mr Sidnell, confession is good for the soul!" I humbly admitted my mistake to the class teacher and the 45 nine year olds. Some time later I noticed she had mis-spelt the word 'manoeuvre' and quietly mentioned the fact to her. The correction was quickly made and if looks could kill, I would not have survived that afternoon!

Another character was the school caretaker, who spent nearly all of his existence in a filthy room making apparently skilled predictions as to the winner at the 3.30 at York. Only a very small part of his time was spent on cleaning. No teacher dared to admit a child had been sick, for clearly he did not regard this as part of his duty. If children felt unwell, we sent them home as soon as possible, as the staff felt that the caretaker would hold them personally responsible!

But Fleetville School was not all bad. I learned a great deal and had opportunities to experiment with ideas of my own. By grading work carefully, I found it possible to keep a class of 48 children usefully occupied. I saw the importance of learning tables, learning ten spellings a day and developing a good handwriting style. On the other hand I quietly dropped such mental gymnastics as: A gross of towels at 1/11 ¾d each, or 961 pen nibs at ¾d each or even, a farmer spent £100 on fencing his square field. Fencing is a shilling a yard. "What is the length of one side of the field?" I felt that the world of rods, poles and perches, furlongs and chains was of limited interest to children having difficulty with addition and subtraction.

CHAPTER 8

Alma Road School St Albans now as a Teacher

John's year of unqualified teaching. 1948 – 1949.
– Prepare to disbelieve!

I cycled into the tiny playground on the first morning of September with a certain amount of apprehension. I had asked the Head if we could meet at his convenience the previous week, but he had very strong views as to what Hertfordshire County Council paid him for. He subsequently informed me that he would be most pleased to help me anytime between 9.00am and noon and again from 1.40 pm until 3.45 pm. "But with no disrespect to you, Mr Sidnell, I am not paid to work outside those limits and I've no intention of starting now". I remembered the school vaguely from when David and I were pupils there at the tender age of eight, some twelve years earlier. It was dark and forbidding then and nothing had changed. Within minutes of being introduced to the Headmaster, he was leading me down a gloomy corridor to my classroom. He whispered "You are lucky Mr Sidnell, you have one of the smallest classes in the school. You have only 43 nine year olds". We reached the solid classroom door. He opened it and there sat before me children in double desks, which tiered upward to the back of the classroom. The children rose and like parrots, sang, 'Good Morning Sir'. I smiled a rather nervous smile and replied. 'Sit down quietly please'. It is hard to believe now that that concluded my introduction to my first class. I turned to ask the Headmaster where I might find the register, but he was already striding into the gloom. One thing was absolutely certain. I would have to learn very quickly or I should sink without trace! "Now I shall require a monitor to help me". A forest of hands volunteered to come to my assistance. In the next half an hour I was shown the new class register, what colour pens to use, where the dinner register was kept, who stayed to lunch and how much they paid. I was reminded to collect National Savings and a very helpful girl even told me I needed to cycle to the nearest post office in my lunchtime to collect the penny and six-penny stamps for my class.

From that very first day, I found the children delightful. This was more than I could say for the members of staff. I was pointedly asked by an elderly teacher who had taught my brother and I years earlier 'And what grammar school did you go to Mr Sidnell?' I informed the shocked teachers that I did not go to a grammar school. There followed what might be called a 'deafening silence.' It was on the tip of my tongue to say 'The Headmistress told my father that scholarships were reserved for the professional classes', but I felt I would have been excommunicated before I had even commenced my career!

I tried hard to be friendly and even asked an elderly teacher if she would 'sit in' on a history lesson I had prepared. She grudgingly agreed. I had painted a picture demonstrating how the Spanish sailors attempted to board the British ships, but were driven back by the English sailors pouring barrels of lime down on the enemy, causing confusion and blindness. The children listened to every word in rapt silence. At playtime I asked the teacher for her comments. She sniffed disapprovingly and said 'Most inappropriate'. As I glanced through the window of the staffroom at the children in the playground, I smiled at several of the boys who were racing round with their hands pressed to their eyes, shouting "I'm blind!'

The year passed quickly and the Head was kind enough to recommend me on the highest terms to the Principal of Westminster College. I was even more surprised and delighted that when the parents knew I was leaving to go to college, wrote letters of good wishes and I even received several bunches of flowers. On reflection, it is most unlikely that students today wishing to attend college, would be expected to cope with over 40 children with absolutely no guidance whatsoever.

CHAPTER 9

*Westminster College – The Great Gamble into Higher
Education 1951-1953*

Westminster College

At the end of the summer both John and I entered
Westminster College through the kindness of the
Principal J S Ross (Jock), on condition that, as neither of
us had the customary fistful of qualifications, we worked
hard and did not disgrace ourselves in the end of term
examinations. We worked very hard, burning the
midnight oil, knowing that our future depended on it.
At the end of the year we surprised ourselves, and
probably the Principal, in gaining examination results
that put us with the top half a dozen students in the year.
At Westminster we enjoyed some lectures and endured

the rest. The lecturers were undoubtedly highly qualified, but some obviously hadn't seen the inside of a classroom for many years and consequently hadn't the faintest notion of how a child's mind worked. Among the best, however, was Dr Shepherd, who had worked for many years in a school in the East End of London. He was quite brilliant and his lectures were well attended, keeping us in fits of laughter with his sensible advice. In those wonderful far off days children could be smacked for bullying, rudeness, laziness and insolence. Caning was usually reserved for special occasions, but not always. As students, we asked Dr Shepherd "How would you deal with disobedient children?" The Doc smiled. "When you are walking between the desks, kick the offending child's ankle hard or tread on his toe, apologising profusely. "After all", he mused "who would believe a child when he said that the teacher deliberately kicked his ankle?" He recalled an incident from his past when he began teaching. At the beginning of the term in a really tough school, he was confronted by a troublemaker who deliberately splattered ink on his neighbour's exercise book, knowing that such an offence was punishable with the cane. Clearly he was out to test the patience of the new master. Dr Shepherd bundled the miscreant to the front of the class and gave him four strokes on his hands and two on his backside. The culprit, in tears and considerable pain, was thunderstruck. Not in his wildest dreams had he expected such terrible retribution. The class had merely expected a 'telling off'. "That", said Dr Shepherd, "was just a friendly warning. Next time you step out of line I shall really punish you!" The ensuing silence, broken only by boy's whimpering, could be felt. There was no more trouble after that!

Above the main door of the college were inscribed

the words from Proverbs, "Train up the child in the way that he should go." Some wit was inspired to write in chalk over the first two letters "Chain up" the child. We were given weekly lectures on Basic Psychology by our venerable Principal. Watching flies crawling up the wall was wildly exciting compared with his lectures, delivered in a broad Scottish accent. It did not take us long, however, to realise his lectures were delivered word for word from his own book. 'The Groundwork of Educational Psychology'. We soon purchased a few old copies and kept half a chapter ahead. When questioned on a difficult concept of his lecture, we were able to give him the best possible answer, 'his own', for which he was absurdly grateful. The notice board advertising recommended copies of such books was directly opposite the Principal's room. Notices as "For Sale— Groundwork of Educational Psychology by J.S. Ross MA (never opened)", must have proved very hurtful to Jock.

Another lecturer, who was brilliant, in his own opinion at least, hailed from Yorkshire. He made no secret of his dislike for "soft southerners", i.e. anyone living south of Birmingham. He was particularly rude to our friend Willis who hailed from the East coast. When, in reply to a question from Dr Oxley, he would commence, "Dr Oxley: I think-" He would be interrupted with, "Its no use you thinking Johnson, you haven't the necessary apparatus".

On one occasion every student was instructed to attend a lecture given by an eminent visiting professor. He was a diminutive gentleman of Mediterranean extraction who rejoiced in the name of Professor Assagiole. The Principal and entire staff were arrayed in their gowns, across the stage of the large theatre. He was given a lengthy introduction and warmly applauded.

His subject was 'The Realm of the Subconscious.' Within a few minutes of the commencement of the lecture it became clear his grasp of the sub consciousness might have been extensive, but his knowledge of English was tenuous to say the least! We students first thought he was speaking in Italian, until we began to recognise the odd word. Our hearts sank as he shuffled through a massive wad of notes. Soon our open note pads began to fill with realistic pencilled sketches of the professor with highly uncomplimentary remarks written beneath.

Another lecturer, a man whose interest lay entirely with his craft, had to be nudged repeatedly to be kept awake. Finally after an hour, the learned gentleman sat down. Our Vice Principal shakily rose to his feet and proposed a vote of thanks. He then made the fatal mistake of suggesting after such a stimulating lecture, we must be anxious to ask questions or seek elucidation on some of the points he raised! There was deadly silence. The Principal looked to his staff for assistance and tried to raise a smile. Most were examining their shoelaces with undivided attention! After what seemed like an eternity, one student, Phil Boreham, stood up and said "Professor Assagiole, I disagree with your first assumption concerning the relevant importance of the sub- conscious." Every head turned to see this Daniel who had dared, not only to speak, but also to question the celebrated psychologist. Before the Principal could intervene, Phil clearly and succinctly gave his reasons. The professor smiled and we all breathed again. Then followed a good-natured exchange between the two. I felt it unlikely that many lecturers followed the points expressed and I am certain that most of the students did not. Finally the V.I.P rose and left. Hardly had the door closed before the entire audience clapped spontaneously to thank Phil, who had so expertly extracted the college from a difficult and potentially embarrassing situation.

Our other lasting memory of Phil occurred when, at the very beginning of our course, the Principal announced that as we should be setting intelligence tests for children throughout our careers, we should ourselves sit one "To know how it feels." He selected the American Otis tests for graduates as being "about right" for our "supposed intelligence". At this point my brother and I could not help but remember the words of the Principal when he first interviewed us. "The students are highly qualified academically, all with O & A levels, some having taken degrees before the commencement of the course." The reader will recall that we had been accepted by the Principal with minimum qualifications; not even a scholarship. He said he would "take a chance' if we did well as unqualified teachers the year before our college career commenced.

I read the first question on the paper, the 'starter question', with utter bewilderment. I didn't understand the question, let alone what was required as the answer! I know it invited the student to fill in the word missing in the sentence 'Evolution is to Revolution as ———— is to flying?' I glanced round and everybody appeared to know exactly what they were doing. I wasn't surprised to see Phil Boreman slip his fountain pen into his pocket after twenty minutes and stroll out. It was, therefore, with some trepidation that we assembled a few days later to hear the results. The Principal gave a short preamble, in which he suggested all students should have scored at least 110 and he expected most would be in excess of 120. He read the results in reverse order. My name was at the top of the list with an IQ of 106! Phil Boreham's was read out last with an IQ of 146! The

Principal was very kind, saying to me, "Ah laddie, you must have had a blank day," inferring that normally I should have done far better. It was considerate of him, but completely untrue. I genuinely could not have done better if I had sat there all day. The realization does nothing to one's confidence at the start of a college career!

It was not all doom and gloom, however. We both realised as we attended daily lectures that we had excellent memories. A few notes jotted down were all we needed to recall the lectures of the day and store them in our minds. Colleagues with much higher IQ's asked if they could borrow our notes and our confidence began to return.

We worked particularly hard, rarely missing a lecture and using our afternoon free period for revision. In those far off days we had two lectures in the morning, one in the late afternoon and yet another before our evening meal. We then retired for at least two hours of private study. Judging by what our grandchildren tell us, often only having two or three lectures a week at university, one can understand why our course lasted only two years!

The other really exciting times from college days were school practices. We loved every minute of these and here, for the first time, we saw the immense value of having spent a year in the classroom as unqualified teachers. We never had a moment's concern as to how or what we should teach. Careful preparation was essential and the fact we could illustrate our lessons both on the blackboard and in our school practice notes, greatly enhanced the results. I used the time when travelling the underground, the 15 stations to Gants Hill, to illustrate my school practice book with my fountain pen, drawing

Elizabethan galleons or Roman villages. I have included two such pictures. Our years at Art schools had not been wasted.

Drawn with a fountain pen on the way to school practice

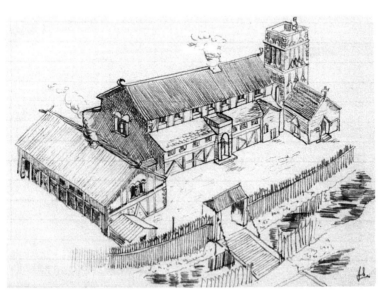

Sketch of Anglo Norman House & a Ship.

CHAPTER 10

John's School Practices.

Within a week of joining Westminster College I was sent on my first school practice. There I joined the staff at Gascoigne Cecil Junior Mixed School, Morley Road, Barking. One of my earliest lessons of one hour was to take forty, ten to eleven year olds for figure drawing. The Head, Mr B.C Wood, sat in on my lesson and, rather immodestly, I have included his comments written in my school practice book. I treasure them to this day.

Headmaster's Comment

This is undoubtedly the best lesson I have heard given by a student practising in this school. It has been painstakingly prepared, and excellently delivered. Mr. Sidnell if proceeding in this way will, I am sure, win distinctions in his College course.

B.C. Wood.
Headmaster.

Headmaster's comments on my lesson.

From that moment onward I knew teaching was for me. At the end of the first school practice, I was asked to write a detailed report on the school. The Headmaster was years ahead of his time. Barking was not an easy area for new teachers. The school had 1100 on roll comprising of infants, juniors and seniors. It drew heavily from the working class area, with three or four children in many families. In most cases both parents were working. Most children lived within a mile of the school. Mr Wood held a Parent Association meeting once a month in order to allow parents to find out what went on at school. It was a great success. Although only two or three children out of forty gained a scholarship, the whole ethos of the school was a revelation to behold.

One afternoon the juniors of any age could join an 'Activity Group'. Here they had the opportunity of learning ballroom dancing, making soft toys, joining a craft group, an art group or a recorder group, with every child playing a tune by the end of term. Also, there was a musical appreciation group and an 'interest group' where invited speakers were asked about their work. In the period I was there, I noted the list of speakers, which included a fighter pilot, a film star wearing a glamorous costume, a BBC announcer, a channel swimmer and a newspaper reporter. When we consider that this was 1949, I venture to suggest that some primary schools have not reached that level of 'real education' even sixty years later!

In complete contrast was my second school practice at Berger Road JM School, Homerton. The school was situated close to the Berger Road paint works and there was also the sound of sawmills within earshot. Almost immediately entering the school I became aware of an overpowering smell of paint and much of my teaching was given to the accompaniment of circular saws! The noise from the market added still further to the 'colour' of the neighbourhood. The school was very poorly equipped and the Head made it very clear that only essential materials were ordered, as there was a strong feeling about 'spending the taxpayer's money on unnecessary luxuries'. Under that heading came physical training supplies, drawing paper and art materials. The children were encouraged to bring their own pencils, pens and rulers and the school was without a wireless! Art drawing paper was never given out, but sheets were torn from a telephone directory and children were encouraged to see how many pencil sketches they could draw round the edges of the print! I felt my tutor's comments on my assessment of the school being 'a little over critical of the conditions' were rather harsh. In the six weeks I taught there, I saw the Headmaster only at the one assembly he took each week and once when I knocked on his door to thank him for allowing me to teach at his school. He didn't get up from his chair, but smiled thinly, giving me the distinct impression he was not aware there were any students in the school.

The school for my final practice was Park Hill Junior School in Ilford, Essex. It was a most enjoyable experience. I had nothing but co-operation from the Head and staff at this relatively modern school built in delightful surroundings. It was well worth the 75-minute travelling time in each direction from Westminster College. The standards of the school were high with the entire 'A' stream passing the scholarship examination, and even 20% of the 'B' stream being offered places. Milk was supplied to all children, but it was noticeable that many refused, as it didn't 'suit them'! On the other hand, the school was particularly well stocked, with every child being provided with a hanger to keep their clothes in proper shape and each child was provided with a pair of plimsolls, which were carefully stored in wire racks outside each classroom. It was refreshing to see the children keen to change for P.E. and games, with boys wearing special shorts and girls in knickers and vests.

CHAPTER 11

David's School Practices – A Baptism of Fire 1949.

My first school practice was at Dorothy Barley Junior Boys School in Barking. I cannot remember, at that point, hearing of, let alone working in, an all boys school. The school was built just six years before the war and was relatively modern. It had large classrooms, separate art and woodwork rooms, and most unusually, a large playing field. The facilities were reflected in the standard of work and sports. Discipline was excellent and restricted to stern words for the lower schools boys and staying in for period of detention for the older children. The pupils took part in a 'house point' scheme enthusiastically, and it was a matter of distinction to be awarded the school cup.

My second school practice was at Marner Street Junior School in Bromley by Bow. Built in 1872, this school was once surrounded by slum dwellings that were completely destroyed by bombing, leaving it overlooking acres of rubble. This was in the process of being cleared when I arrived. On one side of the school there was a wood-yard and a furniture factory. Nearby, the very busy railway marshalling yards made their presence heard. On the other side of the school, forty-foot piles of masonry all but obscured a building that had once been the workhouse. Other places of 'interest' nearby were the massive cooling towers, another railway, and the dock. As the Headmaster so picturesquely put it "My room smells from whichever direction the wind blows". For those interested he would supply the detail. "Either fine sawdust and the scream of industrial saws from the wood yard, soot from the marshalling yards, fumes from the gas works, or the smell of stagnant water from the docks, all combine outside the windows of my school!" The school was constantly invaded by gangs of builders, carpenters, gas fitters and painters. As the radiators were not working, paraffin stoves heated the classrooms, most giving off more fumes than heat. Teaching in this school was to be particularly significant for me. My lesson was to be criticised by the College Principal, my personal tutor, and the resident teacher, all making notes while I tried to teach 45 children about trawlers fishing in the North Sea.

It could hardly have been a more eventful lesson. I thought I had prepared for everything down to a detailed coloured picture of a trawler in a rough sea, which had taken me several hours to paint. I was mistaken. Workmen on the scaffolding level with my classroom windows caused constant distraction. At one stage I felt that the interest of the workmen outside was somewhat greater than that of the children's inside. They frequently stopped work and gave their undivided attention to my lesson. In the middle of a detailed explanation of fishing gear, in walked a workman carrying a bucket of cement. He nodded pleasantly to me and handed the bucket to his mate through the open window. With a murmured apology, he retraced his steps and slammed the door. The VIPs' assessing my lesson smiled encouragingly at me. I continued, but was increasingly aware of a rhythmic banging from above. Little eyes wandered upwards to the ceiling and I began to feel that I was losing the battle. I changed tactics and fired questions to which I knew they would respond. I tried everything to distract them from the knocking, which was becoming louder by the minute. Suddenly there was a tremendous crash of metal from the room above and the accumulated dirt and dust of eighty years descended in a thick cloud, covering everyone and everything. The silence that followed was broken only by a coarse cockney voice of a child in the front row, who in a single word, called into question the parentage of workmen upstairs. The situation was saved when the classroom door opened and an enormous workman appeared, covered in dust and said "Sorry mate, the bleeding radiator fell off the wall!" There was no answer to that! The VIP's rose, shook themselves, and hurried to the door. The Principal made my day by saying "You'll be alright laddie!" Such an experience was rather like undergoing major surgery, without anaesthetic. I sat down and the boys and I discussed Compton's latest century at Lords!

CHAPTER 12

Success at Last

No memories of college would be complete without mention of the wonderful sermons of Dr. W.E Sangster at Central Hall, Westminster. To be guaranteed a seat, it was necessary to arrive there at least twenty minutes early and have the pleasure of listening to Dr George Brockless play Bach Chorals on the great organ. Dr Brockless was our music tutor. For our benefit, he would 'disguise' well- known songs and even nursery tunes in the chorals for us to identify before the Monday morning lecture! College was for us a happy time with many memorable highlights including the college concerts, the inter-college sport matches, and the late evening walks listening to talented buskers in the arcades around Trafalgar Square. We took part in all the college rags while there. On one occasion, John and I walked in procession through the streets of London dressed as girls, with short skirts, black stockings and generously padded bras under tight sweaters and glorious blonde wigs. We carried the poster asking "Which twin has the phoney perm?" They were the days when the 'Toni' perm was all the rage. The only slight problem occurred when we needed to spend a penny. After a brief chat with a watchful constable, explaining our predicament, all was resolved.

Then came the dreaded finals, and we all realized

that there was so much we didn't know. We regretted the extra hours spent in the cricket nets that should have been spent on revision and library work. We studied previous examination papers and realised that some questions reoccurred frequently. We therefore sat down night after night, scanning the questions from the finals papers of many a past year. From these we selected about thirty 'bankers' and worked out mnemonics (aids to memory) from them. For example, the question 'What do you consider the essential qualifications of a school teacher?' This could be answered with mnemonic SHUTAPE, representing the lead words 'sincerity, humour, understanding, tolerance, adaptability, perseverance and, above all, enthusiasm'. A paragraph written on each of these virtues formed the basis of a good answer. John and I were extremely fortunate in being the students to jointly win the College Prize with distinctions for Education, plus distinctions for Divinity and Psychology. My IQ of 106 didn't seem to have ruined my chances of becoming a teacher after all! To all aspiring teachers, if you have a good memory, the battle is half won.

CHAPTER 13

*David's First Appointment – Furzehill JMI, Borehamwood,
A London Overspill School. September 1951*

The expression 'gap year' had not been invented in
1951 when we concluded our two-year course at
Westminster College. A letter I received read 'You have
been appointed to Furze Hill JMI School in
Borehamwood.' At that time Borehamwood acted as an
overspill area for London Schools. My brother and I
attended an interview at the County Hall, where it was
made very clear to us how lucky we were to be
appointed to "one of the best education authorities in
the country". Any thoughts we had entertained to
becoming masters at some quiet village school were
quickly dismissed. At this time there were nineteen
schools in the Borehamwood area. New schools were
built, but immediately extended with huts to
accommodate the weekly increase in the child
population. We did enquire whether we could teach
nearer to our home in St Albans, but our request was
immediately rejected and there would be no appeal.
When we asked how we were to make the eleven-mile
journey, the reply was a very simple 'Get a bus'. John
pointed out, not unreasonably, that the bus fares would
leave little of the £5 a week we were paid by the county.
The gentleman concerned shrugged his shoulders and
the interview was over. The answer was to save up and

buy motorised cycles. I purchased a 25cc 'Cycle Master', which was always breaking down, in spite of the fact that the advertisement depicted a young couple waving happily as their tandem effortlessly pulled them up a steep hill! John bought a second-hand 'Cycle Mate', which relied on a steel cog pressing on the rear tyre. It was crude, but reliable. So often I was waiting at the end of the road where John taught, for him to push me home as my 'wonder machine' had let me down yet again. In the winter we both arrived at school with frozen fingers. This made it hard to mark the attendance register.

Years later, we turned our thoughts again to the method of interview, to which we had been subjected. Clearly the county were simply using anyone to plug the huge gaps in the recruitment of teachers in special areas, but in the longer term one does have to question the advisability of placing teachers with average ability in an environment where, at the very beginning of their careers, they were faced with difficult teaching problems. Children were coming into a new area, and being taught by teachers that were unknown to them. At best, they were likely to be apprehensive, particularly being crammed into schools that were already over-crowded. It was simply deferring the problem, as the authorities must have been aware that once appointed to a school, there was nothing to prevent that same teacher applying for a school nearer to where they lived and probably with less demanding children!

I had very mixed feelings about how the school was run. The classes were large – usually over forty and I received no instruction from the Head as to whether I was teaching as he wanted me to, or not. I was left entirely to my own devices. I do recall that the Head and

Deputy Head vied with each other to finish the 'Times' crossword before morning break, which left me wondering how school administration, and the children in the top class, fared?

CHAPTER 14

St Albans and Real Teaching

Both David and I taught at Garden Fields over a number of years and our 'adventures' are recalled further in the book. However, readers may be interested in what schools looked like in that era. It was probably the most unsuitable place in the whole of St. Albans for a school to be built. It was as if the planners came across a small site near the centre of the town and decided to build there without any other considerations taken into account. The playground, for example was built within two metres of the main road leading into the centre of the town, with the school gates leading directly onto the main road, with only a narrow path between. The school toilets were built on the playground close to the main gates, as far as possible from the school building itself, which meant that any child wishing to use the toilets had to leave the classroom and cross a wind-swept playground. It was always the case in the winter that when the temperature dropped, all the toilets froze and could not be used. The whole school were reduced to using the staff toilet, which was situated next door to my classroom. As the master of that class for five years, it doesn't take much imagination to realise that there was a constant queue of children outside my classroom for most of the day in the winter, with the toilet being flushed almost constantly a mere two metres from my desk! There was a very primitive system of radiators to heat the school and as the school only had one elderly lady caretaker, the pipes, even on the coldest days were never more than warm. This did not affect the Headmaster since his small room was heated by an open fire! During the very coldest months when it was necessary for the children to sit in their coats, the caretaker was ordered to light the tiny oyster stove that did little or nothing to affect the overall room temperature.

I know my brother has mentioned games lessons at the school. Unfortunately enough, the school was situated almost in the centre of a built up area. There was a small area some few hundred yards from the school large enough for some games, but even that necessitated crossing two roads, while the main playing area, shared with the general public, was at least twenty minutes walk away. Many of the lady teachers didn't even bother to walk the distance, but organised games for their classes in the playground. No balls were allowed as any ball thrown a yard too far would end up in the middle of a busy road! The school did not possess a hall, which meant the teacher, unfortunate to occupy that area could not begin his lesson until the assembly was over and his class then had to drag heavy desks from the far corner of the area and conversely drag them all back again at 11.45 in order for the dinner tables to be set up by twelve o'clock! I taught at the school for ten years and I know it was a huge relief to the staff when the school was relocated to an area on the edge of St. Albans, away from town traffic.

I was looking round for a teaching post nearer to St Albans, and to my great delight, I was accepted at Garden Fields School in St Albans itself, at the princely salary of

£7 a week. It was, of course, the old building, but anything was better than cycling twenty-two miles each day! I was immediately happy there under the kindly Headship of Mr A.C Green where, for the first time, I learned what teaching was all about: the daily spelling tests, the formal handwriting exercises, the tables learnt by heart, and the weekly composition marked for content, punctuation and grammar. I soon learned how to be diplomatic with older members of the staff, and even more diplomatic with the parents. I well remember my mother's words when writing reports: 'Speak your mind, but still be kind.'

CHAPTER 15

Cowley Hill, School Borehamwood, 1951.
A Quart Into a Pint Pot

Cowley Hill School Borehamwood

It was with some trepidation that I cycled into the playground of Cowley Hill School for my first appointment as a qualified teacher in 1951. The Headmaster had not been able to see me prior to the first day. There appeared to be children everywhere! This London overspill establishment was grossly overcrowded. Mr Smith, the Headmaster, held out a crumb of comfort in suggesting that conditions were improving and he hoped this would continue in the future. He explained that the main hall now had only two classes whereas previously there were four. Then I noticed a slight hesitation before opening the door of a relatively small room. For a moment, I believed the room would not seat more than twelve children. He coughed nervously and explained that my class 'shared', his actual word, the medical room and the adjacent library. He touched the wall joining the two rooms and in a rather jerky voice muttered, 'I must apologise about the wall though'. Then, and only then, did I realise the full implication of his remark. It appeared I should have my desk 'between the rooms', or to put it another way, in the door space with half the class on one side of the wall and half on the other! He smiled and cheerfully reminded me I came with an excellent college record and a Grade A Teaching Mark and that 'It shouldn't be a problem'. The 'problem', as I soon discovered, was that a child in the library could neither see nor hear the child asking a question in the medical room. I was constantly being asked 'What did she say Sir? I can't hear anything!'

Fortunately, the doctor used the medical room only once a term and then it became necessary to cram all twenty-four children into the library, with strict instructions not to disturb him. When the Head discovered I could play the piano well, the timetable was 'adjusted' to enable me to take all the juniors in the upper school for music. Although this was very popular with the children, the teachers in the hall found it very distracting. I naturally apologised, but one can't ask enthusiastic children to sing quietly!

These were the early days in my teaching career and one of the first lessons I learned was never to show surprise to a child's response to a question asked.

One afternoon in my first term, I attempted to involve the class by encouraging them to tell me about their holidays. I asked if any of them had done anything 'special' in their holidays, remembering this was just after the war and I realised that many beaches were still out- of- bounds, as they hadn't been cleared of mines. Seaside holidays were still relatively uncommon anyway. The response was encouraging and a lively discussion ensued. Then I noticed a small girl sitting quietly at the front, not joining in with the children's recollections. "Come Jane", I encouraged, "surely there's something you'd like to tell us?' The response was a slow shake of her head. I tried again. "Did you go out with your sister then?" I knew she admired her older sister. "No sir", she said, but suddenly brightening up, "but my sister did something very exciting". Greatly encouraged, I asked her to tell us all about it. She stood up with eyes full of excitement and proudly announced, "My sister slept with the milkman last night!" Somehow I couldn't find an appropriate reply to that piece of news! Perhaps the most disconcerting element was what followed. The class began to talk informally about the 'love lives' of their older brothers and sisters and it became immediately apparent that Jane's tale was just one of at least half a dozen similar or even more lurid stories the class wished to tell. I hastily drew the lesson to a close, much to their disappointment, as they found the love lives of their elder brothers and sisters far more interesting than the lives of Roman soldiers in Britain!

Nevertheless, I found the children to be charming and very willing to please. I discovered that they were 'difficult children', according to other members of the staff and didn't fit in with their general schemes of work. By carefully grading their work and giving them lots of encouragement, they progressed, despite predictions, and were very contented. Some measure of the affection that existed between us could be seen even years later: when I had left Cowley Hill and moved back to St. Albans, a party of six girls and boys bussed the eleven miles into St. Albans to hear the stories my brother and I told to a Children's Church each Sunday morning. Even more surprising was that on a cold, snowy morning when the buses from Borehamwood were not running, the same group of children were putting out the chairs when I arrived. I suspected that one of their father's had brought them over by car. I enquired and was stunned at the reply I received from John Thornton. "Oh no, Sir. We walked. We started early and it only took us three hours." I suspect we would not have received the same response from children of today!

I worked very hard at Cowley Hill and thoroughly enjoyed the experience. As you have read, the conditions weren't ideal for a teacher to commence their teaching career, but I was most gratified with the response I received from the children.

As my brother mentioned in the previous chapter he had already discovered a school in St. Albans as he found cycling the twenty-two miles a day too much for him. He informed me a place had become vacant at Garden Fields School in St. Albans where he now taught and he knew the Headmaster would welcome my application. I may say, somewhat immodestly, I am sure he would, having already seen the standard of work my brother had been producing in the two terms he had been there. Nevertheless, I knew I would miss my class and the very full co-operation I received from their parents. The only thing I wouldn't miss was the long cycle ride made each day, particularly having to 'stand on the pedals' to climb Shenley Hill in icy conditions.

I probably disappointed the gentleman from County Hall who had fervently hoped that my stay in a 'difficult' school might be measured in years rather than terms.

It was during my second year at Cowley Hill that I got married to my childhood sweetheart, if one could use this expression today. Because of financial considerations, I was 24 before we 'tied the knot.' We bravely decided to buy a bungalow and by great good fortune my father wished to sell his at the same time. We signed the contract and then found the building society had miscalculated the monthly mortgage. We were tied into paying almost twice the amount we intended. The cancellation charge was a massive £200- quite impossible when my salary was £7 a week! There was only one way out. I took on coaching for juniors in English, Maths and Music after school for 2 hours each night at 2/6, or 12 ½ pence, an hour. I even gave lessons at a private school on a Saturday morning to help my finances and my wife worked as a secretary full time for £5 a week. Those early years were very difficult.

CHAPTER 16

Private Education

I smile when I recall my years trying 'to make ends meet' by entering the world of 'Private Education.' I applied to a private school in St. Albans where I was informed I should receive three shillings and sixpence an hour. I taught for an hour twice a week commencing at 4pm. These were a mixed class of teenagers who enjoyed music appreciation, but definitely not singing! My brother and I also taught woodwork at the same school on a Saturday morning, but increasingly we were faced with late payment of our fees. I saw the Principal and said that we were unwilling to continue in these circumstances. Matters came to a head when the Open Evening drew near. The cheque bounced yet again and I announced we were resigning forthwith. The reaction was immediate. I was shown a beautifully prepared sheet to be handed out at the Open Evening, in which my attention was drawn to my name. It announced 'J Sidnell ACP' (Associate of the College of Preceptors), a qualification I never used. 'Qualified at Westminster College (London University) with distinctions'. The Principal pleaded with me not to resign saying, "On the sheet it claims *Fully Qualified Staff* and you are the only qualified teacher we have!" I was presented with a cheque on the evening when I was asked to make a short speech on 'Modern Education'. I felt sorry for the parents at the school. This was not what private education was all about.

The following day I paid in my cheque to be told there was no money in the account! I faced the Principal yet again to be told "There must be a mistake". Eventually, I was paid out of a shopping purse and asked if I would take 'part payment' in the form of woodwork tools the children used on a Saturday morning! We resigned immediately with the tools. The 'posh' Private School closed shortly afterwards!

CHAPTER 17

David's First Appointment at Garden Fields School – So is this what it's all about?

Being a new boy, I was given the darkest classroom in the school, built in 1912. The ceiling was very high and what little light there was came through a tall sash window starting three metres from the ground. It took me months to learn how to operate them with the aid of a long pole. It was so dark, that lights were obligatory on all but the brightest days. The room was heated by a circular iron 'oyster' stove set in a round base, surrounded by a brass fireguard. This was raked out at 3:45 daily with the accompanying dust and fumes, with little regard for whatever clearing up operations were proceeding at the time.

During my five years spent in that room, the business premises just a few feet away from the classroom window changed hands three times, from a vehicle repair shop, to a car crash repair shop and finally a depot for thousands of tins of crisps. These were thrown, rather than carried, to the waiting lorries. Hence lessons were often disturbed as the children watched with rapt interest as car engines were swung within feet of the classroom windows, or empty tins were thrown on the roof of a specially constructed van. The noise of such operations can only be imagined!

There were some wonderful characters in that school,

both good and bad. In time I learned to decipher such spellings as 'arpsto' which with help, translated into 'half past two'! The pupil, Jimmy, who upon understanding a simple arithmetical concept, would exclaim with delight, 'Gor blimey, so it is!' Another lad was caught in the act of preparing a fire round a petrol pump next to the school. Fortunately he was discovered before the match was struck!

I clearly recall Norman, a likeable rogue, who had crossed every teacher in the school, yet bore no ill will when he was punished. Smacking was a part of school life, as were loss of playtimes and writing long lists of spellings. On one occasion Norman had taken the window pole and slipped it through the 'D' handles of the adjoining girls toilets in the playground block effectively trapping the occupants inside. I caught him and smacked him without enthusiasm, when I should have awarded him a star for initiative. I kept him in for half an hour, while I marked my way through a mountain of exercise books. I was about to send him home when in walked his teacher of four years earlier, Miss Kitty Hall. She had the distinction of thinking well of everyone. Seeing Norman sitting learning spellings with a face like thunder, she smiled sweetly and said. "Oh its little Norman, isn't it? Aren't you a lucky boy to be in Sidnell's class?" I didn't quite catch Norman's reply and in retrospect it was well I didn't! Kitty Hall was a wonderful character, and was at almost retiring age. She was almost as broad as she was tall. She rouged cheeks in bright red spots and looked rather like a turn of the century children's doll. As she lived only a few doors from the school, her more reliable seven year olds were regularly despatched to do shopping or do jobs in her cottage. This necessitated crossing the main road! Such reliable children were rewarded with cash and kind and were guaranteed good class marks! She taught children many useful skills: to read loudly and clearly, to add and subtract and to sit up straight with folded arms! Children reading in her class could be heard clearly on the other side of the playground. I suspected the emphasis on loud and clear enunciation was in part due to her deafness. John's daughter had the distinction of being in her class. Hilary confirmed only recently that she owes her knowledge of tables entirely to Miss Hall, who made her stand on her chair and shout her tables at the top of her voice!

Another unforgettable member of staff was dear Arthur Mills. As he was approaching retirement, and buttressed by seniority, he could disregard many of the passing educational whims. He was invariably 'picturesquely' dressed, often returning late to afternoon school having spent his lunchtime on his allotment. The resulting smell of bonfire smoke would be obvious throughout the afternoon session. We had sometimes to remind him to untie the string he used instead of cycle clips. He was nearly bald and had a pair of thin spectacles perched on the end of his nose. He was, however, a genius at teaching the educationally subnormal children. The other children referred to them as 'loonies'. These days, as we know, they would be classed as having 'special needs'. Arthur was given such children of all ages from the surrounding schools, most of which should have attended 'special schools'. He had not attended dozens of courses organised by experts. His classroom consisted of a dozen or so desks at the end of the hall, where, against all odds he gave his 'misfits' an excellent education commensurate with their ability. His so-called classroom was disturbed daily by the morning assembly, by the school catering needing his space at 11:45 daily, by the school musicals, by the school photographer – the list was endless. His desk at the end of the hall was only yards away from a very steep hill where the heavy lorries necessarily engaged a lower gear. I never once heard him complain and against all odds the children prospered. He wrote them 'secret' messages and hid them all round the hall. When they found them they 'wrote', and here I use the word advisedly, messages in return. They learnt to count in many exciting and ingenious ways. He set up a shop where they bought and sold everyday items. They loved Mr Mills and he encouraged them to produce their best work. Never once in five years did I hear him raise his voice and he always had a quizzical smile on his face. My lasting memory of Arthur is of him calmly undoing his gardening fork from the cross bar of his bicycle, some time after the school had started, with his children crowding round asking questions. In forty years I have never found anyone who genuinely loved and understood such children as much.

As a special treat, my class was allowed to use the latest visual aid, a black and white filmstrip projector. I was fortunate here as the dungeon of my room hardly needed blacking out. We were studying Norman Castles at the time and I picked out 'Norman Castles of England' by A. C. Green. I have to admit the sin of neither reading the notes nor running through the slides before the lesson. Fortified with the knowledge that I knew more about Norman Castles than most eleven year olds, I fed the strip into the machine and put the lights out. I drew deeply on my imagination for all the frames that were not self-explanatory. During the lesson I was aware that the classroom door opened and I called out firmly 'Will the child that opened the door close it immediately!' I ploughed on until a particular frame depicted a torture chamber with an array of instruments of torture – a guaranteed hit with the children. Out of the darkness a little lad called "Sir, what's that iron thing sticking out of the wall?" I hadn't the slightest idea, but called on my imagination and replied that it was a hook to which prisoners were chained. All seemed satisfied. The strip came to an end and I put the lights on. There sitting in the front row was my Headmaster, Mr A.C. Green. Then in a flash I remembered the name on the first frame of the filmstrip. A. C. Green. He looked distinctly bleak. When the children were dismissed he said, "Mr Sidnell, the hook which you so graphically described in frame 11 as being something to which prisoners were tethered, was, in fact, a bracket to hold a torch" I had learned a lesson: always run the strip through first and read the notes!

Every year the 'B' class of eleven year olds had a really worthwhile educational visit, usually a day's trip to London. I did my homework for this and was determined that it would be a great success. I prepared a worksheet for the three venues. The Tower of London, a trip down the Thames, and last but not least a visit to the Science Museum. Perhaps these days, one of these venues would have been sufficient, but these were the times of extreme austerity.

We duly arrived at the Tower, inspected the suits of armour and the dungeons, and sat on Tower Green close to where Ann Boleyn was beheaded, to eat our sandwiches! The children were spellbound when I gave them the edited background to that event. Suddenly, a raven with apparent dysentery, gave my raincoat unwanted attention. Without interrupting the story, I mentioned that if any child found it necessary to remark upon the accident, he or she could take a hundred lines! From The Tower, we boarded a Thames bus to Greenwich and learned something of the buildings, events and people associated with the River. Once back at the Tower pier, the children were counted yet again – forty-eight children, and Mr Green and myself. We then boarded a coach for the Science Museum and for the next two hours the children circulated the floors with us trailing behind. A great attraction was the first black and white television. The children were fascinated watching the Centre Court at Wimbledon. By the time the children had started pressing the buttons on the showcases, sometimes without waiting to see what happened, we decided enough was enough. This feeling was confirmed when one of our little angels found out how to jam the burglar alarm system. On the coach home, the remainder of the food and sweets were consumed with an enthusiasm that made me feel queasy.

I waited until all the children had been collected by their parents and cycled two miles home in light rain feeling utterly shattered. The following day I collected the work sheets from the children and as an after thought asked them to write in one sentence the most memorable event of their day in London. Would it be the block on the Tower Green, the unusual armour, the riverboat or perhaps the black and white television? I was wrong on all counts. Nearly everybody remembered when Barbara Johnson was sick on the coach! I was beginning to understand how the mind of an eleven year old really worked!

The staff at Garden Fields was very contented in spite of Dickensian conditions and there were very few staff changes. The four young men on the staff were all interested in cricket and many a lunchtime was spent on the very rough field behind the Divisional Education offices, taking their frustration out on a cricket ball. We always took a group of boys to collect the ball from the far corners of the field. I have often had nightmares on these occasions. The 'pitch' was rough and uneven. Batting gloves, pads and helmets were unknown. John bowled terrifyingly fast and the ball frequently flew head high from the stony track. He made no concessions whether bowling to fellow staff or children. One little lad boasted to his friends 'I wasn't hurt in two overs with Mr Sidnell bowling flat out!" The law of averages demanded that at least two children should have died playing lunch – time cricket. Yet in all these sessions, I can recall only one accident to a child who was felled by a lightning ball on the kneecap. I felt that congratulations to John by the other boys for a plumb Leg Before Wicket were a little unfortunate, as the batsman lay writhing, and unattended, on the ground. One lunch- time John was bowling very fast to another master, Peter Jenkyns, who taught 3B. Peter struck a ball towards the Divisional Educational Office. We watched in horror as it smashed an enormous plate glass window. It was here that Peter should have been awarded an 'A' for initiative. As quick as a flash his stuck the bat in to the hands of a boy standing near. As he was one of the smallest boys in the year, it was testing anyone's credulity that such a small lad could hit a ball over eighty yards. We took the diplomatic course and sent the Education Officer's secretary a box of chocolates – on behalf of the lad!

We hated football, which had to be played on the nearest public playing field. We could hardly be expected to be enthusiastic after taking a crocodile of upwards of fifty boys on a twenty-minute walk in each direction on a dreary Thursday afternoon. By the time the captains had positioned coats for goal posts, twenty-five a side had been chosen with all the usual arguments, we were left with very little playing time. Much of the remaining time was spent retrieving the ball from packs of marauding dogs that looked forward to their Thursday afternoon game of football. I discovered that retrieving the ball from between the front paws of an enormous German Shepherd required plenty of courage even when its tail was wagging. On their return, the fifty players would discard their mud-caked boots and kit on the floor of the cloakroom, ideally suited for only twenty boys. Another master, who took a lower form, said that in December there would be just enough time to walk to the Heath, where he would kick the ball as hard as possible. The boys and dogs would chase after it and the boy who reached it first would have the honour of carrying it back to school! Some of the local dogs, deprived of their afternoon game, followed the trail back to school. I fully appreciated why winter Thursday afternoons were equally hated by the caretaker, the teachers, parents and by the writer.

The Christmas Concert was the highlight of the year at Garden Fields School. In time – honoured tradition, preparations began immediately after half term. Every class had a free hand to produce an item lasting about fifteen minutes. These varied from nursery rhymes, to fairy tales, to the more adventurous offerings with music, costumes and a few props and scenery. Rehearsals in the hall were a challenge, with the constant roar of passing heavy lorries. The smell of fumes was evident through the ill-fitting windows, often leaving a faint haze at the end of the school hall where a stage should have been. This could have been an ideal scene for a play from Dickens London. A particularly heavy lorry would vibrate dust from rafters in fine clouds. The double doors nearest the stage-end led directly into the playground. During a performance on a wet December night, it was a matter of supreme importance, to time the entrance and exits exactly. On one particular occasion, another wet night, Kitty Hall had yet again resurrected a play entitled 'The Fairies Christmas'. It was copied from a Child Educational Supplement in the early twenties. Any of the senior members of staff could act as prompters as they had heard the play so many times. The infants stood on rickety chairs and shouted in voices that could be heard the other side of the playground, "I am a Christmas tree" and another, stating the obvious, "I am Father Christmas". Somehow the well – rehearsed fairies in their tutus seemed to take longer to dance around the Christmas Tree, with Father Christmas beaming approval. Outside in the rain, patience was wearing thin. Mr Mill's class offering was to be on the lines of St George and the Dragon with, intentionally, no speaking parts. Hardly had the beautifully dressed fairies with their sparkling wands filed out into the driving rain, than Arthur's crew roared across the stage. They were fired up and ready to go! Armed with wooden swords, the odd machine gun and cardboards shields, they set to with enthusiasm.

Never had there been a greater contrast between two consecutive items. Oliver's battle at Agincourt paled into insignificance compared with Arthur Mill's contribution! Old personal scores were paid off and above the noise of the battle, some distinctly uncomplimentary remarks could be heard as St George killed the dragon with a realism that had the parents on the edge of their seats. The dragon's death throes were drawn out and very convincing. Fearing that it would be only a matter of time before someone lost their temper and a nasty accident occurred, Arthur crossed to the centre of the stage and announced "The End', much to the annoyance of some of the lads who were warming to the battle, oblivious to the teacher's command 'to end'. The pirate with the machine gun continued with the murderous round of verbal gunfire. Finally, the parents gave enthusiastic applause, not realising that what they had witnessed bore not the slightest resemblance to what had been rehearsed for the past six weeks. They stood up thankfully, having been sitting on chairs made for seven year olds for two hours. One couple were heard to say as they left the hall, "I never expected anything like that!" I'm equally sure Arthur Mills didn't either!

In nearly all schools, the caretaker is a character. That was certainly so in the early fifties where the caretaker's authority hardly differed from that of the Headmaster! The lady in question at Garden Fields had a short temper, a sharp tongue, and a shrill voice. She worked in all but the warmest weather in a turban and an overcoat. She could not be called a happy person. Most disagreements between the good lady and the staff were caused by lack of cleaning and the lack of heating.

On one icy winter's morning I asked that our 'oyster' stove should be lit, pointing out that we were all in overcoats and most of the children were trying to write with gloves on. I'm glad I didn't catch quite what all her reply was, but it sounded most uncomplimentary. After a considerable time she burst through the door, flung the guard to one side and raked out the ashes. On her second trip, paper and wood were rammed into place and ignited. Minutes later she reappeared with two buckets of wet coke. Immediately dense clouds of white smoke filled the classroom. We all coughed and spluttered and all pretence at teaching was abandoned. Amid the confusion, the door slammed: 'That would teach Mr Sidnell to ask for a fire!' Her only other appearance was at the end of the day when we were finishing with prayers. Such a thing would be hard to imagine these days! The door would be flung open and with complete disregard to the prayers, or me, she would rasp, "Jimmy Windmill, its yer 'at. Don't lose it again!" The hat in question was flung with force and accuracy in his direction and the door would slam shut! Minutes later she would reappear and vigorously rake out the embers onto a steel sheet surrounding the fire, muttering, "This isn't a woman's job!" I would be left with no alternative but to pack up the exercise books, placing them in the pannier of my bicycle and continue marking them at home.

My brother had a similar experience. His classroom had been three days without any form of heat and the children were wearing overcoats and gloves. With two girls actually crying from the cold, John sought out the Head and demanded a fire should be lit, or he would suggest to the parents they should keep their children at home. The Head grudgingly agreed John could light a fire the following morning. By morning playtime, the children were smiling again. By lunchtime they had removed their coats and gloves. Meanwhile, John continued to stoke the fire with great endeavour and enthusiasm. The fire now had reached baronial proportions. By afternoon the children had happily left their classroom 'to get some air'. It was at this point the Headmaster asked John to accompany him to the small pile of coal remaining and bitterly announced that 'Mr Sidnell had used up the entire month's supply which he was keeping for his own room!' John apologised naturally, but added, 'Well at least the children won't be able to get their fathers to write to the Education Officer complaining that they had been sitting without heat for three days.' Somehow this sounded more like a veiled threat than an apology!

All my years at Garden Fields School were spent with 4B, the less bright ten year olds. They were not given a level playing field in which to learn as all the best equipment and books were given to the A forms. My brother spent even longer trying to cope with this unfair situation and will mention his reactions later in the book.

To end with, I would like to note some of the remarks entered by teachers in the child's record book at the end of the term. I hasten to add the first of these was written in a record book in my brother's school. He demanded the entry should be removed, not because he disagreed with the sentiment expressed, but for the lack of tact on the part of the teacher!

- 'With luck she may be able to pay the milkman by the time she is eighteen.'

- 'His altogether admirable effort to help others leaves him little time to complete his own work.'

- 'Martin must try to combine accuracy with speed.'

- 'I'm afraid he is doing his best'.

- 'Roger is an excellent organiser. Perhaps next term his efforts could be directed to his own work!'

- 'Frank is good at impressions; for example, the impression that he likes work.'

It was just as well the report books were given out on the last day of term!

CHAPTER 18

John at Garden Fields School St Albans 1953-1963 – Follow My Leader

Garden Fields Old School St Albans

Garden Fields was a two – stream school, which had an excellent staff with an unusual number of male teachers. There were five men there before I joined which greatly widened the general interest of the staff as a whole. I was, however, unhappy with the two – stream system that virtually picked children to go to the grammar schools at the age of seven. The Head mistress of the Infants school handed the Headmaster of Garden Fields a list of children she thought would be suitable for the 'A' stream and the rest were 'B' stream children. Once in the 'A' stream, the pupils became 'the cream of St. Albans'. They were provided with the latest text- books, which were not available to the 'B'' classes. Towards the top of the school, they were shown scholarship papers from previous years and the teachers of the 'top' class 'coached' the children into the best ways of answering the questions. The 'B' class children never saw such papers or had such opportunities. As a master at Garden Fields for ten years, I taught both 'A' and 'B' classes and was able to see at first hand the huge and completely unfair advantage the 'A' children were given.

At one point in my period of service at Garden Fields, the Headmaster asked me if I would take my own and another class to Alma Road School while our classes were being refurbished. Our 'new' school was, in fact, the one my brother and I attended when we first moved to St. Albans in 1938 and the same school where I taught for a year as an unqualified teacher. It was dilapidated then and had not been used as a school for many years. Audrey, the other teacher, and I were responsible for eighty children between the ages of eight and nine for a period lasting ten weeks. The responsibilities were quite staggering and no Headmaster today would ever consider allowing their teachers to perform such an undertaking. Apart from taking all our lessons, we were responsible for the children at playtimes and at lunchtime. We walked the children in a long crocodile almost a mile to a restaurant, crossing one of the major roads into St. Albans. Here we had to supervise the children's dinners while standing up having our own and then walking them the mile back to school. Under the heading 'Now it can be told' I suggested to Audrey that we took it in turns to take the last hour off each Friday afternoon. Admittedly, it meant the teacher in charge had eighty children to contend with, but as we both could play the piano well, it was no problem. We had a number of 'Thank you' letters from the parents who probably appreciated what we had undertaken more than the Headmaster had!

As the years went by other men on the staff got the promotion to Deputy Head and even Headships. I decided I had served my apprenticeship as an assistant master and began to look around for Deputy Headships.

CHAPTER 19

Skyswood JMI School 1963 – 1966 – What a lovely School!

Skyswood School St Albans

The years at Garden Field School flew. By the end of ten years the Headmaster had given me experience at teaching both 'A' and 'B' classes. It was when I was teaching one of the last 'B' classes, a child, Sharon, joined the school. She was nine and it was obvious that she would benefit from 'A' class teaching. I daringly approached the Headmaster with the suggestion she should join the 'A' stream for the last year. I received reluctant agreement from the Head and open hostility from the top class teacher! It was, however, finally agreed. I was surprised to read in a local newspaper recently that Sharon remembered her spell in my class over half a century ago. She wrote "I was nine when I became a member of Garden Fields in 1958 – not an ideal age to orient oneself to new study methods for eleven plus, or to fit in with new pupils and a new teacher! Any concerns I had were dispelled on my first day in Mr Sidnell's class. His respect and consideration for children was extraordinary. He was a great story teller, inventing tales of magic and treasure and at home-time we begged him to continue and tell us what happened next!"

Sharon had coped well with the 'A' stream work and by the end of the year her examination results testified to it. I was right to move her from the 'B' stream.

Gradually, however, as all my colleagues left for promotion, I realised there was no further advancement at Garden Fields as the Deputy Head made it clear she intended to retire from that post. The post of Special Responsibility, worth £50 a year, was shared between the five men on the staff, so I had £100 in my ten years at the school, for which I was responsible for all the music at the top end of the school, the choir, the recorders, the football and cricket. I was also expected to take the children on various outings.

The First Step on the Ladder

Thus began a period when I commenced to make applications for Deputy Headships in Hertfordshire. I was short listed for some schools, but there were many disappointments. I was, however, learning what to say with each new interview. It was clear one had to be completely honest and a quick thinker. I recall I was once asked by an elderly lady on the local Education Committee if 'I would allow the top class boys to dig my garden?' I was very shocked at such a suggestion and fortunately the Education Officer quickly made it clear that such work did not come within the remit of the duties of a Deputy Headmaster! He apologised profusely afterwards, but I was not offered the post.

Then, quite by chance, I discovered a Deputy Head I knew well had been promoted to Head of Skyswood JMI School. I applied for the post there and, to my delight, I was short-listed. Four applicants were interviewed. I had set my heart on the post, for this was an excellent school in one of the best residential areas in St Albans. I was the last to be interviewed and, judging by the smiles on the committee, I guessed I might be lucky this time.

Of course no encouragement was given at the interview, but when I was offered the post, the Headmaster murmured, "What kept you?" We shook hands and I had taken the first step on the ladder. Mentally, however, I assured myself it would not be another ten years before I applied for a Headship!

As the Deputy, I was given the top class of ten and eleven year olds. The school was a one-form entry, which meant mixed ability classes. I had certain ideas I wished to try and here was an excellent opportunity. I believed the segregation of 'A' and 'B' classes was not a good idea. I found the brighter children acted as stimulus and also promoted healthy competition within the age group. It was obvious that the children who were brighter with basic work were not always those who showed enthusiasm for subjects just as important in a 'well rounded' child. I encouraged those with an artistic ability and exhibited their work round the main school areas. Children who could sing were encouraged to sing at assemblies and it was in this school I introduced a cup for special achievement. This idea, when developed, proved to be a match winner, but initially it was just for the top class. My idea was not to give it to the most gifted children, but rather to those who were polite or who had made a real effort with their work. I pressed the idea of school uniforms and pride in appearance. It was to have a dramatic effect upon the class and even the less academically inclined saw that what they were able to achieve was regarded as equally important.

At the same time, however, I wanted to encourage the obviously gifted children. To that end we had a lesson which encouraged them to extend their vocabulary. It was so successful that those interested, mostly girls, I'll admit, begged me to continue in their playtime. As a special favour I allowed them to sit on their desks and as a mark of appreciation, one of the groups would always walk down to the staffroom and bring me a cup of tea. The game was played by giving the group a word – for example, 'custom' and then I would challenge each child to give me another word, which in some way, they could associate with the word I gave them. To begin with I wasn't too strict, as the name of the game was encouragement and having a fun time. After moments of thought one girl said 'mannerism' and explained how she would associate that word with 'custom'. The reader will quickly appreciate I had a group of very intelligent children, who enjoyed the challenge. I was always delighted with their response and made such comments as 'Really, I had no idea you knew such difficult words'. It worked like a dream and spurred them to try new words. In that particular game, a girl surprised even me, coming out with the word 'idiosyncrasies' and making real effort to show the relationship with 'custom'. We all clapped her and even the Headmaster, who had wandered into the classroom, wondered how the children had heard these words. Finally, a boy asked me if 'eccentricity' might be a strange custom. I saw his thinking and he received a clap from the group and some admiring glances from the girls!

I also introduced a book for English homework entitled 'Harder Vocabulary Exercises'. Each page contained twenty sentences with a selection of vocabulary beneath. The child had to place the correct word in the sentence to make sense. The reader will appreciate that this involved a great deal of marking. I always had over forty children in my class and most completed the questions, thus leaving me with over eight hundred sentences to mark on a Thursday night besides all the maths and essays. My long-suffering wife remembered 'Thursday nights' at Skyswood School many years later! This became the right night for her to go and see her parents! One parent once told me that the telephones were very busy with parents comparing answers! Again that didn't matter, as it gave them an indication as to what I hoped their children would achieve.

It was becoming clearer every day that there are almost no limits to what a child can reach, given the right incentives. At Skyswood, their enthusiasm was a joy to behold. I usually wrote play parts to suit the children. In learning parts for plays, bright children regarded it as a challenge. I recall a mother coming to see me, asking if I would speak to her daughter who, having been given a major part in the play, rushed home every day and ran upstairs to her bedroom, refusing to come down for tea until she had learned 'so many pages' – word-perfectly. The mother said any protests were always answered by, "Mr Sidnell said," 'as if you were next in line to the Almighty". I gently explained that I had given her a major part in the play, but as rehearsals didn't commence for three weeks, I'd be quite happy if she knew her part by then. Her father was so relieved, a few days later he knocked on my door and handed me a parcel containing the latest long- playing recording of 'Hansel and Gretel', explaining he had seen it in a record store on Broadway, New York and immediately thought of me! A lesson I had well and truly learned: parental support is a huge factor in the development of the child at school.

I have to say how much I owe to the Headmaster of Skyswood School. He in no way restricted my teaching, but allowed me to experiment with ideas and different approaches to education. I was sorry in many ways that I was offered my first Headship just three years later. I enjoyed the daily contact with enthusiastic children of all abilities and with imagination it was possible to integrate a whole range of class activities, to everyone's enjoyment. There was never any feeling that some children were cleverer than others. The emphasis was on each child doing their very best and being rewarded for their efforts rather than blaming them for their shortcomings. After all, if a child is working to the best of their ability and obviously cannot do more at that stage, it becomes pointless and frustrating to accuse them of not doing their best. I believe I first became aware of this when I was a pupil at Beaumont School during the war. The master showed us one example of long division of money and then proceeded to cover the board with questions for us to solve. When I asked for help or advice or offered an answer to a question, the master would make some unnecessary remark to me in front of the class like "That, Sidnell, is a stupid question. Perhaps this will sharpen your dull wits" and I would receive one cut of the cane. All it did was to increase my inability to think sensibly and such questions as £37,429. 16/- 6.¾d divided by 39 had no place in everyday life. Mention must be made of my idea for class projects in the top junior class. We began by talking about their genuine interests and I emphasised I wasn't going to give gold stars for pages copied from reference books in the school library. I wanted them to write their own thoughts not plagiarised from other school material. I told them that I discovered I learned a great deal by listening to what my parents and grandparents could tell me. My grandfather had an excellent memory and enjoyed telling tales of his boyhood in the reign of Queen Victoria. I gave the class a fortnight to produce a folder of work! Naturally the standard varied greatly. Some produced, perhaps ten pages of straightforward facts, while the brighter third of the class vied with each other in all sorts of ways. Perhaps to better illustrate their project with pictures or with the help of mum and dad, take photographs to clarify a particular point. Many children became so 'involved', they begged for more time to finish work to their satisfaction. One girl I remember particularly well. Her name was Lynda Purfield. She decided to write a book on the 'English Countryside'. She assured me she had 'so much more' to write in her quite exceptional handwriting, she needed more time. At the end of a month, I was of the opinion Mr & Mrs Purfield had a right to see their daughter and not expect her to rush in after school for an evening of study in her bedroom. Her hours, days and even weeks of genuine research confounded me. Finally, she presented me with a ringed folder of over 200 pages of what I would describe as original work, which would not have disgraced a project undertaken by an intelligent sixth former. By great good fortune, we were able to meet again very recently and she confirmed she still has her 'English Countryside' over 45 years later. The final page contains my comments and three gold stars I awarded her for her masterpiece.

I have particularly happy memories of that class. Some children came in before the whistle to finish off work, while my class monitor ensured the register was placed neatly on my desk with red and blue pens ready for use. Other monitors checked my cupboards were tidy while others placed piles of homework on the back seat of my car ready for marking.

My whole experience at Skyswood was one of extreme satisfaction. Interestingly I was asked by the present Headmaster to attend the school on the occasion of their 50th Anniversary celebrations. Readers will recall I was appointed Deputy Head there from 1963 to 1966. I was delighted to see so many of my former pupils, now in their fifties, coming along to share the memories of their years at the school. One mother related how she surprised and delighted her children in showing them the correct way to catch a cricket ball, a skill I had taught her all those years ago! Another gentleman surprised me by telling me what my favourite piece of classical music was-Brahms Variations on a theme by Haydn, The St. Anthony Choral. I found it quite breathtaking what they still remembered fifty-five years later! Even after half a century, in my mind, I still hear that top class begging me to continue after the bell, as they were interested in the lessons or a story I was telling them. Even 'throw away' remarks they remembered; a solemn warning to today's teachers!

I contrast that with my first day as a qualified teacher, when I was shown my class and then left without any knowledge of what was expected of me. I wasn't even shown how to mark the register. I contend that no teacher should be faced with such unnecessary problems on the first day of their career.

CHAPTER 20

Killigrew School – David – A Case Of The Willing Horse?

Killigrew School

After five happy years spent at Garden Fields, I felt it was time to move on with future promotions in mind and by sheer chance a new school was opened within a quarter of a mile of our home. I applied for the job and was accepted taking the upper juniors. The building was everything that Garden Fields was not; well planned, light and with classrooms overlooking open fields. The Head left me very much to my own devices and I was able to transfer all the ideas that were successful at Garden Fields to Killigrew. I found out that the school was named after Killigrew, a famous British admiral. Why more of this was not brought to the children's notice I shall never know.

In the early days, the many faults in the construction of the school had begun to show themselves. I usually arrived first at school and one morning I found a huge sheet of glass cracked and in danger of falling on the hall floor. The school was very exposed and in the winter the driven snow quickly piled up round the main entrance, sometimes delaying the opening of the school door at 9.00am. When the Headmaster found out that I had made bookcases at home, he lost no time in requesting, not only bookcases, but shops, post offices, and display units for the whole school. The list was endless and mounted by the week. The Head greeted me regularly with the words, "Ah, Mr Sidnell. I was wondering whether you've had time to make the post office for the top infants?" It was more than regrettable that our second child was unfortunate enough to sleep like an angel most of the day, but made her needs known from about 7pm to 3.00am, after which we all dropped into exhausted sleep.

Having read what my brother has written about his early days at Killigrew School, I am of the opinion, however biased, that the school hugely benefited from his undoubted talent at woodwork. The units were constructed most professionally with mortise and tenon joints and would last the school for decades! David was offered the cost of the wood for the joints, but not a penny for his undoubted skill.

David continues, I took over the training of the cricket team, which was, for me, a most enjoyable job. It was not long before a cricket table was laid, when my friend, the local groundsman, made it the envy of most primary schools. As if to gild the lily, a parent with connections to a local cricket club, asked if I would like a heavy roller. I readily agreed, but was quite unprepared for what was rolled off a lorry by several strong men. Clearly this was meant to be pulled by a horse! The boys were delighted to be harnessed up to drag this enormous roller over the pitch until it was as flat as a proverbial pancake. The Head didn't say much, but I felt that he regarded the episode with certain misgivings. It was clear after year or so, apart from being awarded a 'special post' worth about £50 a year, there was little chance of a real promotion.

This, I regarded as less than generous on his part since I had made it my responsibility to oversee so many projects which had proved to be highly successful right from the start of my teaching at the school.

One amusing incident, however, does remain in the memory. After I had been there a few months we were all informed that permission had been given for the firm who supplied and built all the ceilings in school, to take photographs throughout one day. Accordingly, photographs were taken of all the classes dancing, enjoying PE, having lunch, listening in assembly, and playing in the playground. Nearly all were low angle shots, taken to show to advantage the ceiling tiles. It seemed that wherever one went, a man with a camera was lying in wait. At the end of a long day when all the staff was heartily fed up with the photographers, I kept a lazy boy in after school. As I was leaning over the child pointing out the unsatisfactory nature of his exercise book, the classroom door opened and yet another photograph was taken. I was not best pleased. Later the Head explained that all the photographs had been taken by Bowater's, the firm responsible for fitting all the ceiling tiles and they advertised nationally. I wondered if they had decided to print any of the photographs. Would it be the children dancing in the hall, undertaking

P.E or making cakes, I wondered? A few days later I had my answer. My photograph leaning over the indolent ten year old appeared on the front page of nearly every broadsheet in the country. A friend of mine remarked, "If you had committed murder you couldn't have had a bigger photograph". Later, another friend produced a copy of the Readers Digest with the same photograph prominently displayed. As an aside, he mentioned that the monthly circulation was thirty two million copies!

David at Killigrew School Teaching.

It was not long before I began to wish heartily that I never joined the staff of Killigrew School. Our house seemed to be a beacon for every parent of children in my class who never let an opportunity pass but to enquire about the progress of their child. I was almost afraid to work in the front garden until the sun went down. The final disappointment came a while later when I looked out of my classroom window to see bulldozers tearing up my cricket pitch. No one had thought to tell me that a new infant's school was to be built on the pitch!

CHAPTER 21

Oakwood School Primary School St Albans
– Wheels Within Wheels

Oakwood School

While glancing through the Times Educational Supplement, I found that a post was vacant at Oakwood JMI School. I also noted that my very good friend, Peter Jenkyns was the Headmaster of this new school which opened a few months earlier. I applied and was appointed to a class of upper juniors. There began almost twenty years of teaching, the happiest years of my life. If I had an interview I don't remember it. It was probably something to do with the fact that Peter and I had the same high standards and we shared the same sense of humour.

Soon after I arrived plans were drawn up for a

swimming pool and all the fund raising plans were explained to the parents. The pool was to be sixty feet by twenty-five, complete with changing rooms and a heater. The total cost was £1600. The parents organised sales of every kind and the money came rolling in. Many of the dads gave up their weekends for the heavy manual work and we were told not to enquire too closely when lorries laden with cement, sand, timber and aluminium railings appeared. The great day arrived and the pool was opened by Millicent Martin of 'That Was The Week That Was' fame. The Mayor, the County Educational Officer and other officials were amused at Peter's witty remarks. No mention was made of the occasion just prior to the opening when I filled the pool with 35 thousand gallons of water from the nearest hydrant, leaving the neighbourhood with greatly reduced water pressure. As the pool could be heated, it was extensively used by the P.T.A for evening and weekend swimming. It was not long before most children at Oakwood had earned their 25yd-swimming certificate. Indeed, the school invariably did well in the local primary school swimming galas. Some time after I retired I was disappointed to hear that the pool had been filled in. Is it feasible that this was done due to the increasing cost of maintaining the swimming pool?

The Deputy Head left and was appointed to the Headship of a nearby school and I was appointed to fill that position. Peter and I worked well together and I was given every encouragement to experiment with ideas not listed on a time- table. I always found the Open Evenings very tiring and there were some occasions when I was talking to parents at midnight. Years later, the evenings became even more demanding when I found that I had to persuade disgruntled parents that their child was not obvious university material at the age of seven!

A New Interest For The School.

One evening our eldest daughter was holding up Smokey, our cat, to look through a toy telescope. I had a look and was amazed to see craters on the moon. I brought a three inch refractor for the school and we had a few evening classes when we took it in turns to moon gaze. Even parents caught the bug! At home shortly afterwards, I set up a telescope I had purchased. It had a ten inch refractor and I had made an observatory with a slide-off roof for it. I'm afraid my family didn't take kindly to being hauled out of bed at 2.00am on a winter's night to see a double cluster in the constellation of Perseus!

I had to do my homework to keep up. One lad produced a notebook on Astronomy that many sixteen year olds would love to claim as their own. I sent it to Patrick Moore and received a congratulatory letter in return. After the project had been going for some weeks, I had a request from a parent to discuss 'an interesting project' with me. Mystified, I arranged to see him. He explained that his lad was so interested in astronomy that he would like to present the school with a telescope! I found out he owned a large construction company and such a gesture was entirely genuine. Clearly, he was not aware just how expensive a good telescope could be and I had to tactfully tell him that a really good professional three-inch refractor could cost over a hundred pounds. I waited for his reaction, which was not long coming. "I'm not talking about toys. How much would a professional 4.75 inch refractor cost?" My mind raced! "It could cost over five hundred pounds!" "Good" he breezed, "we'll have a domed observatory at the same time". I thanked him profusely. Clearly he had real money to spend. In those days I did many things without reference to Inspectors or the Divisional Education Officer, but I hesitated and rang our DEO to discuss the matter. I'm glad that I did. He intimated that a beautiful refractor would be acceptable, but advised against an observatory quoting planning regulations. I'm sure he was right, as my successor would have been bequeathed something in which he very likely had no interest. I was delighted to receive a magnificent refractor complete with every conceivable accessory including a motor, which kept the telescope in exact rotation with the stars. The children and some parents spent many happy evenings stargazing. I even brought it home some weekends and marvelled at the power and clarity of the instrument. In bright sunlight at full magnification, it showed clearly a damaged nut on a structure half a mile away. I have wished so many times that I had offered to buy the telescope when I retired. My successor sold it within weeks of being appointed.

My door was always open to staff, children and parents. Every Friday afternoon I had a trail of children outside my room sent by teachers to show me their work, whether it was a five year old who had written their name for the first time or an eleven year old who had written a poem. At 2.30 I usually had a few children who needed to be told in no uncertain terms that their work or behaviour was not good enough and 'sir 'would be watching him. I soon found that being a 'Head' was not only rewarding but also demanding. I was responsible for everything and everybody – children, staff, cleaners, and cooks and to make matters more interesting, the governors meeting held each term. I was fortunate in always having governors who supported me on every occasion. Virtually all the problems occurred due to differences between the cleaning and the catering staff. One cleaner usually arrived late and was aggrieved with me when I said that I couldn't, in clear conscience, sign for time that she was not working in school. There were a few grumbles and protests but my criticisms were accepted. Later that term I was told that many of the cleaning activities once done as a matter of course were no longer permitted. I began to wonder if caretakers were permitted any cleaning duties! When the caretakers post become vacant, I was pleased to appoint on the recommendation of another Head, a "willing, hard working Irishman"

The Vanishing Caretaker

Indeed his willingness and application to his job could not be faulted. He was always industriously working well before his official starting time. There was no criticism of his work from the cleaners or the staff. To enhance his small salary I suggested that he might like to be responsible for the heating and maintenance of the school swimming pool. He was delighted and I carefully explained the importance of the purity of the water. This was achieved by adding carefully measured quantities of white powder every morning early and then with the aid of simple colour code instrument checking the results. The temperature of the water was taken and where necessary adjusted. He appeared to understand the instructions with many "Yes sir", "No sir", "I understand sir", as the case may be. Thus he began his career as 'Pool Maintenance Officer'. Within days I had a visit from the County Pools Maintenance Officer. He brought to my attention that all the important safety levels were dangerously wrong. My willing little Irishman had been dipping liberally into the very expensive tubs of white powder and with gay abandon flinging the contents all over the pool. I had a serious talk with the 'wee man' who admitted that he "Hadn't quite got the hang of it yet!" I monitored his work for a few days and all seemed well. At the next visit from the County, I was asked to accompany the officer to the pool. I could hardly believe my eyes. The gentleman from the county said mildly as clouds of steam rose from the pool, "I've had colder Turkish baths than that!" How long the pool heater had been at maximum I don't know, but I promptly ordered another five hundred gallons of oil to ensure that the temperature of the school came nearer to the temperature of the pool. The little Irishman had a look of bewilderment on his face and a few days later asked if he could have a few days leave of absence as his mother was not expected to live much longer. I immediately sent him on his way. He mounted his cycle and with profuse thanks, called over his shoulder, "7.30 Monday morning, Sir". He vanished off the face of the earth!

I was very fortunate in having several excellent secretaries. One can survive for a while with an indifferent teacher, a useless caretaker, but without an intelligent and competent secretary, the school grinds to a halt within a few days. Heads these days need to employ three secretaries where I employed just one. By far the best, however, was my sister- in- law who I already knew to have all the qualities of a first class secretary. Doreen was skilfully diplomatic with staff and parents alike. I never gave the routine work a thought as it was all processed with speed, accuracy and without fuss. Her talents ranged far outside her office where she was accepted by staff and parents alike. I never ceased to congratulate myself on having such an outstanding secretary. Alas, for me, John, as Head of a much larger school than mine, needed her talents as his secretary. I've never completely forgiven him for stealing the most efficient person at Oakwood School!

Do We Lose Peter?

Peter the Headmaster, was a man of many talents, but above all he was a superb musician. He was equally at ease conducting the Primary School Festival, conducting the local operatic society or writing songs that juniors loved to sing. It was hard to see a man of such outstanding talents as a Headmaster of a junior school for very long. One day he confided in me that he was applying for the post of County Music Advisor – a post for which he was ideally suited. The resident occupant was retiring and saw Peter as the obvious choice. Unfortunately, he didn't get it and we were all disappointed for him. Instead he applied for a music post at a Teacher Training college and was indeed appointed. I was able to act as Deputy Head until advertisements could be circulated. I was given the unenviable task of showing applicants round the school and generally answering questions. They came in smart cars, complete with brief cases and asked endless questions about the running of the school. I felt as helpful as a messenger boy. Hence I could hardly believe it when I found that I was on a short list of six.

The five applicants and myself were summoned to the County Hall. Compared with the others who were either Heads or, in one case, a lecturer at a training college, I felt very much the odd one out. The interviews lasted about forty minutes each, when all manner of questions were fired at us by seasoned Heads and County Dignitaries. I remember little of the interview except that they persisted with their questions until they were fully acquainted with what I would do in my most difficult school situations. At the end I was mentally and physically exhausted. Nevertheless, to my great surprise, I was offered the post. The family were delighted and there were hugs in the staff room when I gave them the news.

I was fortunate in having a staff I liked, comprising several exceptionally talented teachers. All were determined that good basic work should come first and foremost. My top class teacher trained the netball team who won the primary school cup with monotonous regularity. When a member of the staff was leaving, usually moving out the district, it was a matter of supreme importance to find a good replacement, before the Divisional Educational officer insisted I took on a first time appointment. On one occasion a friend of mine telephoned to recommend a young lady moving into St Albans area. I arranged an interview and together with the chairman of the Governors appointed her for the following term. She proved to be an outstanding teacher who produced a series of maths books to help children make the change over to metrication. I heard later that the DEO had another post in mind for this teacher. By then she had already been appointed to my school. He was not best pleased with me.

We usually made our mark on the sports field due in no small part to the dedication of the teachers and indeed some of the parents, who regularly trained the children in after school sessions. One eager governor offered to coach the high jump team for the local sports. He worked hard with his selected group and I had high hopes that the boys would attain the necessary height of 3'6". On the sports afternoon one lad jumped 4'3" and the other 3'8" easily winning the competition!

When appointing new staff one made every possible enquiry, both official and unofficial, to ascertain their strengths and weaknesses. I received several favourable applications for a post in the lower junior school and one young lady seemed eminently suitable. The applicants were questioned by two governors and myself and as I suspected, the said lady was the best teacher by a long way. As I had several teachers moving for good reasons, leaving the district or getting married, I was determined that should I appoint this lady, trusting she would be with us for a few years. These were the years when one could be undiplomatic without repercussions. After the conclusion of the interviews I said in a half joking manner "I take it you haven't considered started a family yet?" The answer came immediately. "Should I be fortunate enough to be offered this post, I would hope to be a valued member of your staff for many years to come!" We all breathed a sigh of relief and the chairman offered her the post and she accepted it with alacrity. I was not disappointed in my choice as she quickly settled down and both her progress and the children's behaviour were highly commendable. Towards the end of the first term, I received an early morning phone call. I was always at my desk before 8.00 am. It was a request from the recently appointed teacher to collect her from home, as her car had broken down. I collected the teacher who thanked me many times on the journey to school. As she stepped out of the car she smiled and said in a matter of fact tone. "Oh, by the way I'm pregnant!"

I rarely had to punish children except for rudeness, or sheer disobedience. A slap on the side of the leg was all that was required. I can't remember a boy re - offending. Indeed, a verbal reprimand was, in most cases, all that was necessary. I can recall giving a boy an uncomfortable time in my office for stealing sweets. When I sent him back to his room suitably admonished, the adjoining door to the secretary's room opened and she said" I don't know how Robert felt, but you nearly had me in tears!"

I like to think that as Headmasters my brother and I reached a happy compromise over corporal punishment. When we ourselves attended Secondary School the boys were caned on every possible occasion without thought or consideration. We saw, in so many cases, this form of punishment accomplished very little. On the other hand, if children know in advance that nothing can be done in the way of punishment, this can only breed contempt for school authority, and perhaps authority in general. Besides, punishment reserved for special occasions, has far greater effect.

CHAPTER 22

Hertfordshire Schools, Cuffley Camp

Cuffley camp

We both usually took our schools to Cuffley. I pen some of the features of that week.

The very idea of taking up to forty juniors to sleep under canvas in the middle of a wood for a week, must at best seem misguided or courting disaster. In reality, nothing was further from the truth. The camp was situated in the middle of Northaw Great Wood and had been used by the County for many years. It consisted of a number of independent camps set within a few hundred yards of each other, with tents for girls and boys, a large marquee for communal activities and the obligatory camp – fire area. Each school had a completely free hand to organise what activities they wished and plan an exciting week for the children.

John well remembers the first occasion he took a party of forty children to Cuffley. The children were physically big but quite unused to walking through woods. One day the party left camp before 2pm and John pointed out various trees and they listened to bird songs. By 3pm a proportion of the heavier children complained they were tired. John reassured them that they were 'nearly there'. In fact he had completely lost his way, but by some happy chance at about 4pm he heard the sound of a distant car. He immediately headed in that direction with his party of very weary children. An hour later he recognised the road, but it was on the far side of Cuffley Woods! The party eventually arrived back at camp with promises of a 'special camp fire' and a long sing – song. The children enjoyed their sing – song, together with some 'extra rations' supplied by the camp warden, but by 9pm, all were fast asleep!

Some schools simply took their children for walks in the woods each day and accompanied the school down to the main dining hall for a prepared meal. We saw this as completely unnecessary and cooked all our meals over the camp – fire. Naturally the children were expected to collect dead wood from the forest and after dragging it back to camp, set about with saws and axes to cut it up. I'm sure today the idea of allowing children to hack wood with sharp axes and saw through thick trunks with bushman saws would not be encouraged! Discipline was easy, as points were awarded for the honour of sharing the silver cup for that day. An incorrectly folded blanket or a piece of litter the size of a postage stamp was enough to ensure that the tent did not receive the cup around the camp – fire that night.

The children filled in their diaries each night and on occasions these made hilarious reading, making it hard to believe we were in the same camp! On occasions fires were so intense that they did not need relighting the following morning! We were on excellent terms with the camp warden (not warder, as the children liked to say) and he invariably called in for a glass of cider on his nightly patrol.

Without supervision some children would not have washed for the whole week. There were compulsory morning washes and in the evening a lady member of the staff supervised the girls and we supervised the boys. These were the occasions when talcum powder was worth its weight in gold. There were always a few children who were homesick. The tried and trusted remedy for this was plenty of hard work of the most enjoyable kind. It never failed. The same children on the Friday were the first to be asking, 'Can't we stay on for a few more days sir?'

Thursday night's campfire was the high light of the week, when every school was expected to sing an item round the communal campfire. The best was awarded the Camp Cup, a great honour! These offerings varied enormously in skill and content. In John's rarefied academy, they frequently offered beautifully rendered two part songs accompanied by treble and descant recorders, while the others sang songs that would not have been out of place at the 'Nag's Head!'

I recall an incident that wasn't funny at the time, but raised many a smile later. Most boys relish climbing trees and one year David took a diminutive lad to camp. He was extremely agile and more at home thirty foot up a tree than on the ground. One morning a message came from the camp warden to ask if he might bring a group of dignitaries round at 11am, as they were considering starting camps in their counties. At the appointed hour the warden approached to give them a tour of David's camp. They asked questions about safety with the children using saws and axes and particularly tree climbing. This was forty years before Health and Safety dictates took nearly all the fun out of camping. They were about to depart when, high above the clearing, a happy voice called, "Can I climb any higher sir?" There, forty feet above the clearing, swinging on an extremely thin branch was our 'tiny friend'. David suggested he should find a thicker branch nearer the ground and he immediately did as he was asked. The warden hastily reassured them he was happier in the trees than on the ground and they departed! That evening the warden and Dave had a good laugh over the incident.

As we took the children to listen to the nightingales in the wood long after dark I found many campers didn't like wandering too far away from 'Sir' They would wake each other up and go to the latrines in pairs. These affairs were for emergency only and were pretty primitive. I was awakened in the early hours by a group of boys who informed me that 'Robert had dropped his torch down the latrine'. I opened my eyes and said, "What a pity" They departed somewhat disappointed!

On one occasion John was overseeing activities at the campsite when an older boy from another camp wandered onto the site, Silver Street (each of the school camps were given a name; we always requested Silver Street as it was in the deepest part of Cuffley Woods). He shouted a story about a lion being loose in Cuffley woods. His accent indicated he came from northern England. On hearing this, John's assistant teacher jumped into her car, which happened to be parked nearby, with commendable haste! The rumour seemed to be confirmed when a jeep raced across the camp with two men, one wearing a bush hat and the other with a coil of rope in his hand. Suddenly, the boy pointed behind John into the woods with the words "Look, there's a lion there!" When he looked round what he actually saw was a 'line' fastened between two trees. His accent had made the 'line' sound like 'lion'. John heard later that a lion had escaped from a circus the other side of the wood and had been captured.

As you will hear later when I became Headmaster of Brookmans Park School I still continued to spend a week every year at Cuffley with my wife helping me to cook daily meals for forty children. With that number I also took a member of the staff. I think it would be fair to say that many children from Brookmans Park had not experienced camping quite like Cuffley Camp. I do recall one girl, however Angela, who was so reliable that I broke the school rules and took her on successive years, really to show the third years just how camping was done. My wife and I were always up before six, to find Angela had already been for a wash and was preparing breakfast. Her spirit of adventure was sorely needed when, as often happens, we had heavy rain and the mud came close to the top of the children's Wellingtons. I recall that on the Friday, when we used the mini bus to ferry the children back to school, we often asked parents to assist with the transport. One parent, Megs Wilson, declared she had never seen such conditions and could hardly believe the children could be so cheerful. One mother came to see me the following Monday morning to explain that her daughter had slept almost all of the previous forty-eight hours. When she appeared on the Friday afternoon straight from camp, her mother made her go round to the back of the house and remove every stitch of clothing which she then dropped into the dustbin! I had to apologise to several parents who said their daughters were so frightened at the late night stories I told them round the camp fire, that they refused to sleep by themselves at home and insisted they slept in their parents' bed. I did agree, however, that this was a great deal to expect of them.

I recall on another occasion when the children from Brookmans Park had only just arrived and I was at full stretch organising children who were clearly not used to this kind of existence, a girl, dressed immaculately in white jodhpurs, a neatly ironed white blouse and spotless white plimsolls and ankle socks, wandered from her tent and requested very politely, "I'll have my coffee now Mr Sidnell". To her credit, she realised that she had overstepped the mark and immediately apologised!

The children at Brookmans Park were bright, but physically on the small side. They wanted to play a game before the camp- fire commenced. They decided on cricket and selected a boy and a girl as captains. They picked sides and I was pleased to see a mixed team. The girl captain was a natural leader and asked if I had any bands they could use to identify their teams. I said I hadn't. The girl said 'Don't worry sir, I know what to do.' She returned to her team of boys and girls and ordered them to strip to the waist. There was absolutely no hesitation from either the boys or the girls and an excellent game was played. On reflection, I was glad I didn't make the suggestion!

CHAPTER 23

The Conclusion of David's Headship.
Oakwood Primary School

School life was full of surprises, nearly all pleasant, but my enthusiasm for school left me with less and less time for my family and for myself. Almost before I realised it, Oakwood had taken virtually all of my life and my health began to suffer. Normally I am a very fit person but asthma attacks and sleepless nights began to sap at my energy. The doctor gave me some inhalers for the asthma and advised me to delegate more of my tasks to others. I would arrive home at the end of a long, tiring day and immediately fall asleep on the settee. Finally, I was persuaded with great reluctance to contact the County Medical officer, expecting him to advise me to take a few days off to recover. How wrong was I! After a prolonged medical he gave me no alternative but to retire at the end of term, only a few weeks away. This came as a complete surprise to my colleagues, friends and the family. For the last few weeks I put in an appearance in the mornings, took assembly, signed any vital letters, gave a few necessary instructions to my deputy, who was a very capable lady, and drove home for the afternoon. I had no difficulty sleeping for the next eighteen hours. The last week passed in a blur; feverish activity to produce our Christmas concert, hosts of goodwill letters from parents and friends and the final farewell gathering when many kind things were said about me by the DEO, and Chairman of the Governors. I was presented with gifts from everyone from the children up to the County Education officer. Perhaps most heartfelt was a Victorian Silver tea service with the teapot stuffed with twenty pound notes. It was with much sadness that I said goodbye. I retired after twenty years at Oakwood. The medical advice proved correct, for it took over two years to be even partially free of asthma.

Now thirty years later, I have a store of many happy memories and life is never dull. At times I even wish I had a class of eager smiling faces waiting for the next lesson!

CHAPTER 24

Success at Last – My First Headship.
Kenilworth JMI School Borehamwood. 1966-1973.

Kenilworth School

We have been writing of those occasions when David's school Oakwood and the school where I was Deputy Head, Skyswood, were at Cuffley Camp together. I wish to take the reader back to Skyswood when I commenced applying for Headships. I had only been a Deputy for two years and appreciated that I really hadn't enough experience, but there was no harm in trying. At an early interview for a Headship the Divisional officer took me aside afterwards and said encouragingly, "Keep the applications coming Mr Sidnell. It's only a matter of time and experience."

Then within a year of my first application for a Headship I saw a post advertised for a school in Borehamwood. To my surprise, the current Head was a master I had worked with at my first school after leaving college. He had been the Deputy head at Cowley Hill School. Kenilworth was a very light, open school and he explained he had a very supportive staff. He was sure I would be happy there as a first Headship. I applied and was delighted to be short- listed. My present Headmaster congratulated me, but had hoped I would have stayed longer, a sentiment I could well appreciate.

I am sure all young prospective Heads are nervous at such interviews. I know I was. I was asked to explain in some detail how I would develop the Parent Teacher Association. Here I was able to describe to the governors some of my experiences at Skyswood and show how closer contact with the parents brought its undoubted rewards. I went on to explain that in my previous school, I had made a series of slide presentations, showing as many aspects of school life as possible. This clearly interested them and I was questioned closely as to the part the parents played. The five hopeful candidates waited anxiously for the Divisional Officer to appear. I remember his words as if they were yesterday! "The committee have had a hard time making what proved to be a difficult choice." Did that mean we were all pretty awful, I wondered? He continued, "The committee, however, have come to a unanimous decision to ask Mr Sidnell if he would be willing to accept the Headship." Naturally I was delighted and my hand was shaken by the DEO, Governors and, with somewhat less enthusiasm, by the unsuccessful candidates. I was particularly sorry for one of them who announced in the waiting room, that he was the Deputy Head and had been on the staff, by all accounts, for twenty years and fully expected to be offered the post. To his great credit, he offered me his full support and in return, I felt I should give him as much responsibility as possible. Before the term commenced I asked him if he would order some toilet rolls. He obviously felt privileged to undertake this task and promptly ordered twenty boxes for which I signed the requisition slip. On the first day of the term the caretaker had stacked the boxes at the end of the hall. When I saw them, my heart sank. The boxes reached the hall ceiling! Each box contained not fifty rolls as I thought, but two gross, making 5760 rolls altogether! I did not order any more for the next four years, but the general account took a year to recover!

It was true I was learning all the time, but as a new Head, I had no experience in dealing with staff. I felt it a great shame that some 'pointers' were not discussed at college. I appreciate this would be looking years ahead, but a glimpse would have been useful. The other thought that crossed my mind was that it did seem strange that, apart from Heads of small schools where the Head is also a teacher, one is appointed largely on the grounds of their teaching ability, yet much of the time is given to administration which I knew nothing about and on which, truthfully I wasn't particularly interested. A three-day course was arranged for all new Heads in Hertfordshire, but I am ashamed to say I cannot remember a single word of advice given! Yet, strangely enough, my earliest problems at Kenilworth concerned the caretaker. One of the soundest pieces of advice given to me by a colleague was "Look after your caretaker, particularly if they are good. A good caretaker is worth two teachers!" My problem occurred when a member of the staff, who should have known better, allowed his boys to tramp through the hall with their muddy football boots. The caretaker was rightly annoyed as he prided himself in his highly polished floors in the school. I had previously told him his floors were better than those at the Science Museum in London before the war. I apologised and ordered extra polish out of school funds, which I considered a small price to pay for an excellent caretaker. Very shortly after he complained he had done extra work for which he had been authorised, but now the County refused to pay. He told me he was considering getting a new job! This I could not allow. I rang County Hall directly. There was no way I was going to lose an excellent caretaker due to their stupidity. I spoke to the officer in control of Caretaking finance and informed him I was backing my caretaker to the hilt and was quite unwilling to leave this impasse. He agreed to pay the money the county owed immediately. I wanted this matter settled, so I told the officer that the caretaker and I were travelling over to County Hall that morning. The finance officer offered the caretaker a full apology and we all shook hands and cups of coffee were produced. I drank mine without thinking, but got only as far as the car before my hands began to shake uncontrollably. My legs were also beginning to make involuntary movements. I began to sweat and then I remembered my doctor advised me not to drink black coffee! The caretaker drove me home and a doctor was fetched. Fortunately my condition improved by the end of the day, but I had learned my lesson!

I did have an occasion to speak very seriously to a member of the staff whose teaching methods were open to question. I entered her classroom to find a group of children round her desk being skilfully taught the elements of reading. This, I wholeheartedly approved of, but glancing round the room, I found it practically deserted, for the rest of the class were busily throwing buckets of sand at each other in the sandpit! I pointed this out to the teacher who surprisingly said she was busy with the readers and couldn't at the same time be responsible for 'the periphery'! I suggested that twenty-five children could hardly be described as the 'periphery' and in the final analysis it would be me who was answerable to the governors for any accident which occurred to unsupervised children. Clearly, we were not looking at the problem from the same perspective. At the end of the school year she joined another school where her specialised knowledge could be used to full advantage in dealing with small groups of children.

One of the main sources of employment in Borehamwood, beside the sellotape factory was A.T.V Studios. Very early in my headship one of my fathers, who worked at the studios, introduced me to the lighting director, telling him he had seen my Christmas productions and was amazed at the standard the children had reached. Thus began an association with the studios, which lasted until I retired from Brookmans Park some seventeen years later. A visit to the studio was like a visit to Aladdin's cave. I was almost embarrassed at what he had to offer: props, scenery, and the sort of lighting and effects probably only seen at a London Theatre. The reader will readily understand that a 17 way dimmer plus 12 spots and 12 floodlights are not within the grasp of many primary schools. Together with this, there was as much scenery as I could have wished for, both painted or blanks on which I could exercise my artistic skills. All of this, plus many special effects as required for a full-scale production, were delivered both to Kenilworth and to Brookmans Park Schools. I include some early scenery I painted for a play at Kenilworth school.

Backcloth to the play- Early Hansel and Gretel.

I often took over from a class teacher doing playground duty as I found I could learn so much just by watching the children playing and having casual conversations with them. One young girl approached me and volunteered; "My dads in prison sir and my mums got a new boyfriend!" She spoke as if she was asking the milkman for an extra pint of milk! I found the parents also were willing to discuss their marital problems with me. I soon believed it was easier to include the Social Services in these discussions, otherwise I could easily have become an unpaid care worker as well as a Headmaster!

On another occasion when I was on playground duty I noticed a girl standing apart from the others in her class. On enquiring what the problem was, she told me the other girls were being nasty to her. "Why is that, Beryl?" I enquired. She tearfully explained that the other girls say I'm wearing a 34 inch bra, but I'm not. My bra is 36 inch. Look sir, I'll show you". She was trying to lower her dress. I said rather hurriedly that I believed her and didn't need any confirmation of the fact. She smiled and said she'd tell the girls 'You believed me.' I was relieved she didn't say, "Mr Sidnell said my bra was size 36 inch!"

On another occasion my secretary asked if I would take a private call from a mother. I picked up the telephone and I could tell by the tone of the voice that she was tense. "I'm going to end it all Mr Sidnell." she announced, "I can't live with this pressure any longer. My husband has left me and it's all down to me to look after the kids". I suggested that we should talk before she made any decision she might regret. I walked quickly to my car. Then I had another thought and returned to the staff room and asked a lady member of staff to accompany me. We arrived at the house and rang the bell. Almost immediately the lady in question opened the door with a smile on her face. She was wearing a pretty see- thru nightie! Her smile froze when she saw the lady member of staff walking up the path. Without stepping over the door, I suggested she might get in touch with Social Services for help and advice. How pleased I had second thoughts before leaving the school gates. I was learning fast!

To me assemblies were the highlight of the day. It was here I could mould the aims I wished for the school. I made up stories with a strong moral content. In my view stories read from a book means that vital eye contact with the children is lost. Eye contact is also essential throughout the assembly. I was fortunate enough to play the piano to a high standard and I naturally introduced the "Heads Cup." This idea I brought with me from Skyswood School, but now I was able to include the whole school. The emphasis was on good behaviour and consideration for others. The winner placed the cup, together with their name printed below and the reasons for the award, in the cabinet in the entrance hall. Parents were invited to read the achievements of their off- spring and the entire school applauded the winner enthusiastically.

One lesson I learnt many years later concerning my assemblies. I had an e-mail, from a boy who was in the school when I first joined. I took a small party of boys to a science exhibition in London that proved most enjoyable. On our return to Borehamwood, the boys were collected by their parents. The following week at assembly I gave the Head's Cup to one of the boys I took in my car to the science exhibition. I said he remembered to say 'Thank you' to me when he was collected. The person who sent the e-mail was not that person, but another boy in the car. He wrote saying he felt awful just walking off and not thanking me. He said he vowed it was a lesson he would never, ever forget. He went on to write he was now married and had two teenage daughters and he impressed upon them how guilty he felt all those years ago and they must make up for their father's error! In one sense there's a salutary lesson to be learnt here by all prospective teachers. One never knows how long your remarks are remembered by your class!

A Teacher's Worst Nightmare – A Missing Child!

It was during my first Headship that I learned to expect the unexpected. However well a programme is planned, one can never quite cover every eventuality. As I mentioned earlier, cricket rather than football was my game, but it would have been silly not to encourage an interest in all games. I therefore decided to take a coachload of boys to a Schoolboy International at Wembley Stadium. It was England versus Germany. I persuaded a lady teacher to accompany me and we took forty boys. It was an excellent game enjoyed by all and at the end we marched back to the coach park where literally hundreds of coaches were waiting. We found ours eventually and began counting boys back on the coach. The lady teacher could only count thirty-nine! I checked and she was right. I left her with the coach and retraced my steps to the ground. I searched in vain. Soon there remained only a handful of boys left outside and it was obvious my boy was not there. My teacher rightly reminded me we shouldn't wait too long as the parents waiting at the school would become anxious. I informed the police, giving a full description of the boy, his name, our school and my home telephone number. We waited another fifteen minutes and then I told the driver to head for home. On my way I rehearsed what I should say to the parents and of course, I should return to Wembley in my own car. Back at school a crowd of parents were waiting for us and there, standing in front, was the missing boy with a man holding his hand! On enquiry it transpired the man was the boy's uncle who had also been at the match and seeing the boy, had offered to bring him home in his car. The boy, equally stupidly, agreed and simply left the party without informing anyone! The reader may gather I made my views very clear to the man for such a thoughtless action and I demanded the boy's father should meet me in my study at 8.00am the following Monday morning. At that interview I made it clear that his son would not be included on any future school trips. Had the father offered any sort of apology, I may have reconsidered my decision, but the man simply shrugged his shoulders and left my room without a word. My talks at assembly that week all centred round the theme of 'consideration for others and the need to say sorry!'

The years at Kenilworth passed and in the seven years I remained Head, I was conscious of learning what the duties of a Headmaster really were. I had great support from the staff and the parents. I was, however, beginning to wonder whether I should apply for a post at a bigger school in another area. I recalled my predecessor's words when I was appointed. "This is an excellent school to learn your trade." Then, out of the blue, a colleague from another school in Borehamwood enquired whether I knew my school was designated to become a First School with the children leaving at the age of nine? I was devastated by the news. The whole of my teaching experience had been centred round producing well -adjusted children at eleven, to begin their secondary education. I spoke to the Divisional Officer who sympathised with my predicament and advised me to apply for other schools in his division that retained children until the age of eleven.

Accordingly, I started applying for other schools and almost immediately I was faced with a dilemma. I was short listed for a Headship of a school on the outskirts of St. Albans, which I quite liked, but just days before the interview, I was also short listed for a large school some miles from St. Albans, which in all honesty, I preferred. A visit to this school confirmed that would be the answer to my dreams! The school was situated in what might be described as 'stockbroker belt' and had an enthusiastic staff. It was close to delightful countryside and possessed a large swimming pool. I learned that this had been built by a very forward-looking P.T.A.

The day of my interview to my first school approached and I lost many hours of sleep pondering my best course of action. Should I accept the Headship of the first school or take a chance I might be offered my dream school? The first interview went well, but I still had an unresolved question in my mind. After the interview, the Divisional Officer met the five candidates with these words. "Gentlemen", he said, "We have a problem. The committee are undecided whether to offer the post to Mr Sidnell or Mr ——". [His name, I confess I forget.] "We are holding a Special Governors meeting here next Monday to decide." My heart jumped! The interview for my dream school was the coming Friday! From that moment I focused all my attention and energy on the school at Brookmans Park.

CHAPTER 25

The One I Wanted, Brookmans Park School- 1973-1983

All the applicants were invited to Brookmans Park School, and the Head, who was retiring after twenty years, showed us round. In the conversation with all the other applicants, one thing became obvious. They were either Headmasters of other large schools or, in one case, a college lecturer. Nobody was going to be handed this school without the most careful scrutiny! Each applicant was interviewed by the Board of Governors for 40 minutes and I was last to go in. To the unenlightened, this can be an extremely nerve -racking experience. With answering so many questions, one has to be completely honest and if possible, think about why the question is being asked. I was asked what my future plans were for the school and particularly if I saw the advantage of a Parent Teacher

Association? Here I was on very safe ground and was able, in ten minutes, to give a fairly comprehensive overview of what I hoped to do at Brookmans Park were I invited to become their Headmaster. I wanted them to see that while encouraging the brighter children, I should be particularly keen to promote the education of the 'whole child' and was happily able to give examples from my previous Headship. I was thanked for my answers and returned wearily to the waiting room where we all sat very nervously for another twenty minutes. Eventually, the Divisional Education Officer opened the doors and uttered those never-to-be-forgotten words: "Thank you all very much gentleman for being so patient. After due consideration the Governors have unanimously decided to ask Mr Sidnell if he would accept the post as Headmaster of Brookmans Park School." I just couldn't believe what I had heard! What followed turned into moments of unbelievable euphoria. I was conscious of the DEO shaking me warmly by the hand, followed by the other candidates. Next the Governors came forward to add their congratulations. It all seemed so impossible, so unreal, until the DEO said, "We mustn't keep Mr Sidnell from the most important person who should be told. Please use the telephone to give the news to your wife." He indicated the Headmaster's room. I stepped forward and walked through the door, closing it quietly behind me. It was at that moment in time my mind travelled back to the original film I once saw of "Goodbye Mr Chips". Chips had been invited to become Headmaster of Brookfield School. It was something his wife, Kathie had always said to him, "One day, you will be Headmaster of Brookfield School". Now I was Headmaster of Brookmans Park. Somehow, it seemed absolutely right.

I sat for a moment in the Head's chair before lifting

the telephone. I heard my wife saying, "Hello, this is Doreen Sidnell." There was a long pause and then she guessed it was me. She waited and in a hushed voice I just said just three words "I've got it". Typically she whispered, "Oh darling, I'm so happy for you." Her voice broke and I knew she was shedding tears of joy. The dream school was mine.

Brookmans Park School from the air.

As I left Brookmans Park that morning the DEO bid me goodbye and said "I assume you are not going further with the Headship you were offered earlier in the week?" He didn't smile and we never mentioned the previous interview events ever again, but I sometimes wondered whether I was a part of the plans for his division!

My first meeting with the Parent Teacher Association was one of those occasions I shall not easily forget. Here were parents who were used to "thinking big". They were from the top professional classes, as bankers, doctors and captains of industry. One of the first questions I had to answer was concerning the ways I would use any money they raised. I had done my homework and explained one of my first aims would be to buy a long wheel base mini bus. I explained I would take children to concerts in London, to Cuffley Camp and to all sports fixtures. The treasurer asked the approximate cost of such a vehicle? I said that a nearly new one would cost £10,000, but added hastily that I appreciated it would take a considerable time to raise such a sum. The treasurer said he liked the idea and would contact me when he had something to report. In less than a year the money was raised and I was handed a cheque for £10,000. Even better, one of the parents offered to negotiate a good deal for such a vehicle. I soon discovered there was always a pool of willing helpers for Jumble Sales and of course, Village Day. This event was not just the main fundraiser for the school, but also for the village, since any organisations could hire tables for a few pounds and sell goods for their own charities. As an added draw, the school paid for the main attraction. It was a common sight to see up to a thousand people gathered on a hot Saturday in June. The Village Day Queen was voted for by the school, together with two maids of honour. It was the ultimate honour for a girl to be chosen as Queen.

Village Day Queen and Maids of Honour

By 5.30p.m, on Village Day, an army of dads would be taking down the stalls and clearing the field. The day's activities usually ended with a grand dance in the main hall which gave the ladies a chance to show off their latest creations and enjoy a well deserved drink or two with the men. On the Sunday morning a band of dads helped me to clear the field and the last traces of Village Day. The result was the school always had money to spend on extras for the children.

Of course as in all schools, there are high and low points in the year. I recall a particular low, soon after I had been appointed. The P.T.A always arranged the village firework display to be held on the school field. It was a grand affair and even in the early days, more than twenty- five years ago, often £400 was spent on the display. On one occasion the bonfire was lit too close to the school where builders had been invited to dump all their combustible materials. By the evening it had reached gigantic proportions. Unfortunately, it was lit by an eager parent and within the hour, two parents with hose pipes had been detailed to sprinkle water on the nearby glass windows to prevent them from cracking! On another occasion a box of air mines had been left uncovered and a stray spark fell into the box. In the following minute the crowd, fortunately watching from the other side of the field, had the alarming sight of eight air mines heading towards them, instead of bursting harmlessly in the air hundreds of feet above their heads! It was indeed a miracle that no one was injured, but I did have some explaining to do the next morning to the Chairman of Governors! I had to guarantee that the following year all fireworks would be kept away from the firing area and secured in boxes until the moment of detonation!

There was, however, a downside to my way of running the school and something I could do nothing about. Evidently the parents liked the 'old fashioned' methods with the emphasis on basic skills and placing an interest in the children taking pride in their appearance and showing consideration for each other. New families began moving into the catchment area of the school and their children were entitled to be accepted there. Class sizes grew. Thirty-five to forty was the norm with several classes over forty and at one time there were 52 children in the top class! This was only possible by the Deputy Head giving each section of the class different schemes of work to accomplish in a day. It also meant I taught the class several times a week to enable him to attempt at least some of the marking a class of that size involved. I recall I met him leaving school very late one afternoon with 52 maths tests under one arm and the same number of compositions under the other. He smiled and remarked that he expected to be finished well before midnight! The dedication of the staff was quite extraordinary and it was shown by the results obtained. The headmistress of the Grammar School complained that 'I was doing her 'no favours' as my girls were at least two years ahead of other primary schools in the district'.

There were other innovations, which appealed to the parents. Before a child joined the school as 'a rising five', I invited parents to a meeting at the school. Here I spoke to them in the main hall, while their offspring were introduced to the reception class teacher. I used a party of responsible top class girls to accompany the new children. They always did their job with great understanding and I was truly proud of them. I allowed time after the talk for any parent to see me in my room on any personal matter they wished to raise. I recall one such interview. Both mum and dad came in and sat down. Dad leaned forward in a most conspiratorial manner. 'We have a real problem,' he began, looking to his wife for support. 'I went to Christ Church and my wife went to Lady Margaret College. We were wondering whether you could recommend a college for Lucy?' I took a deep breath and said gently, 'My aim is to give Lucy the very best possible start to her school career. I don't think at this point in time we want to speculate as to the most suitable college for her.'

There was very little need for punishment at the school and I only gave one boy the slipper in ten years and then I immediately rang his mother to explain the very unusual circumstances. I simply said that her boy had completely lost his temper and I caught him trying to force the head of a nine-year-old girl down onto some metal coat pegs. It was fortunate I was passing at the time, to prevent what could have been a serious accident.

It was at this school I was able to implement what I considered to be a 'whole education' for the children. Using the large mini bus, I was able to take large groups of eleven year old children to the Ernest Read music concerts at the Festival Hall on a monthly basis. My wife always accompanied us and took the responsibility of caring for the girls in the group. This provided her with an excellent opportunity to get to know the girls informally and forming friendships which often lasted for years after they left Brookmans Park School. This proved most successful and we often had a waiting list. I recall what could have been an embarrassing situation on one such visit. I reminded the children to go to the toilet before the concert. My wife accompanied the girls while I waited for the boys. I decided to wash my hands while I waited. Unfortunately, I entirely miscalculated the force of the water from the shallow basin, and before I could step back, most of the water had been deposited over the front of my trousers, giving a very realistic impression that 'sir' had wet himself. In a situation like this one had to be honest. I warned the boys about the power of the water and to their credit, no one smiled. The girls were just as good, but it did not, however, stop almost every child running to their parents when they arrived back to school, giving a graphic account of the 'wetting of Mr Sidnell's trousers!'

The School Swimming Pool

We were fortunate in being one of the few primary schools to possess a swimming pool. This had been built by enthusiastic parents in my predecessor's time. I decided the 'season' could be further extended by using P.T.A funds to erect solar heating panels on the roof of the changing rooms. We always seemed to be fortunate in having dads who were experts in fields of work required by the school. They all gave generously of their time and energies for projects such as this.

I wrote all the parts for the Christmas production during

the summer holidays and by October I began to paint the scenery. This acted as a huge spur to the children's interest in that they all wanted to see how far I had got with the backcloth when they filed into the hall the following morning for assembly. I include a very early rehearsal of a scene I painted for 'The Sleeping Beauty'.

The rehearsal of the Sleeping Beauty

I particularly enjoyed taking groups of children to see special shows. I recall taking a large group of top class children to Saddlers Wells to see a wonderful production of Humperdinck's fairytale opera, 'Hansel and Gretel'. It was such a visit that fired my enthusiasm to put on a full-scale production at the school. Here again, I was able to compliment the school's resources with massive help from my friends at ATV studios in Borehamwood.

They were able to supply me, not only with huge canvasses on which I could paint scenery, but unusual touches, which made the difference between usual primary school productions and a really professional play.

I began writing my interpretation of Hansel and Gretel in the summer holidays, so I already had a good idea who would be offered each part, covering about twenty-five pages of foolscap each and I expected the whole play to last just over one hundred minutes. I had the whole range of ATV lighting at my disposal including the seventeen way dimmer board plus as many flood and spots as I required.

Sir's Production.

I ask the reader to visualize just one scene from the play. This is where Hansel and Gretel are lost in the forest. The scenery depicted a woodland scene, stretched across the entire stage with free – standing trees to add depth to the view. The children had fallen asleep and were guarded by fourteen beautifully dressed angels. Here again all members of the staff gave me a degree of support I had no right to expect. Many of the mothers gave their time and expertise to dressing and making up the cast. Imagine Hansel and Gretel stirring with just a glimmer of dawn beginning to light the stage. Morning mists were produced with a smoke machine and leaves rustled across the stage. The dawn chorus can be heard faintly at first and then gathering volume as the rays of sun make pools of light on the stage. Hansel and Gretel are asleep against a log in the centre of the stage scene, but as the sounds of birds increase, Gretel stirs and looks around her. She wakes Hansel, but he is unwilling to stir. While the focus of attention is drawn to the main characters, the scene-shifters slowly raise a black net curtain, which divides the front, and back of the stage and low back lights reveal the witches house with smoke curling from the chimney. I made the house to have an upstairs storey so the beautifully dressed witch could appear from behind a curtain drawn across the top window. I chose the witch with great care. She was a highly intelligent girl, whose acting ability would not have seemed out of place in a senior production. When I first saw what an expert job one of the mothers had made of her costume and also saw how professionally she had been made up, I decided to take her down to the reception class one afternoon before the final rehearsal to the school. I wanted to 'break the ice' as it were, before the infants saw her on stage. Even though I was careful to introduce Grania to the class of five year olds, there were several anxious moments when she peered into their startled faces. She was beautifully made up with her face tinged with a dull green and with very realistic long black fingernails she grasped their arms. The tension was broken only when she offered to have a brave boy sit on her lap!

Woodland Scene- Hansel and Gretel,
behind the Chairman of Governors.

My enthusiasm was matched by the children who ordered their parents not to call for them until 45 minutes after normal school time on rehearsal afternoons. I smile when I hear some educationists preaching that children should not be 'pushed' and not too much expected of them at the tender age of eleven. It was all done with everybody wishing to give it their best and it was so refreshing to hear children asking to rehearse parts again they thought could be improved. I rather felt for their parents who had been sitting in their cars waiting for their offspring to appear, to be told when they stood at the back of the darkened hall, 'We can't possibly come yet. Mr Sidnell's got a problem!'

I recall how I used to ask a member of the staff to watch a scene of the play when I needed some critical evaluation. Many was the time poor Ann Childs appeared at the hall door to listen to the choir or sit through a scene of a play when she should have been on her way home! It was the feeling I always had that the staff were backing my endeavours that, in no small way, encouraged me to try out new approaches and ideas.

I always thought it well to let the parents see what was going on in the school. Whereas it was not possible to allow parents to stand at the back of the classroom with the teacher at the front, once a year I made a slide show and invited parents for an informal evening when it was shown. Much amusement was caused.

Once I began the evening by saying to the parents "Before we begin, I'll make a pact with you. I promise not to believe all the children tell me about what goes on at home, if you promise not to accept every word as gospel truth of what you hear goes on at school".

Most children lived in lovely houses and when one nine year old was describing his house to the class, he couldn't remember whether it had five or six bedrooms! The reader will realise that Brookmans Park had some very desirable residences.

I recall taking written English with the top class and speaking to one particular girl whose writing on 'Exciting things I have done' rather disappointed me. She appears to have some ideas, but these hadn't been translated into good English. She was a clever girl and I knew she was capable of a great deal more. I said encouragingly 'Can you make up a story about the ponies you have in your paddock at the bottom of the garden? She didn't think that was particularly exciting. "What about the heated swimming pool you have?" Again she looked doubtful. I tried again. "I happen to know your father flew down to Bristol in his own aeroplane last weekend. Could you describe what you saw from the window?" She thought for a moment and said "I didn't see anything sir, I sat in the back and read a book!" Then quite suddenly she brightened up and said, with real excitement in her voice "I know exactly what I'm going to write about". I enquired what this could be, remembering she had turned down the ponies, the heated swimming pool and the flight in her father's aeroplane. "I'm going to write about the day my gran took me to London Zoo on the bus". I rest my case!

One day, the father of the girl who was so fortunate, knocked on my door and presented me with a beautifully mounted aerial view of the school. I was completely overwhelmed with such a generous gift, and promised it would take pride of place in the entrance hall. He hesitated and looked at me with real surprise. "Do you mean you have never seen the school from the air"? I had to admit that I had not had the pleasure, thinking to myself that I couldn't believe there were many

Headmasters in Hertfordshire who had had that privilege either! "We must do something about that John," he said "Could I meet you and your good lady wife here next Saturday morning, weather permitting and please bring your camera"? The following Saturday, the parents drove up to the school in their white Rolls Royce and the four of us drove to the local air -field where his aeroplane was waiting. We flew over St. Albans and I took photographs of the Abbey and even our bungalow. My wife and I were thrilled. We enjoyed the flight immensely. Some parents might have taken advantage of the situation to ask after their daughter's progress at school. Her name was not mentioned.

We landed and then he had another idea. "Could you meet us next Saturday and please bring your passports?" "Yes, we would love to", Doreen breathed before I could say a word. I wondered what adventure he had in mind. On that Saturday we had lunch in Le Touquet and afterwards explored the town and did some shopping. Yes, Brookmans Park was a very special school!

My wife ran a Care Centre in St Albans for over twenty years and she suggested the older children might like to visit the old people of Brookmans Park at Harvest time and bring harvest gifts. As this was my first Harvest Service at the school I decided that I should take a party of children to meet some of the 'needy' people in the village. We had prepared tins of fruit, flowers and vegetables in baskets and the children would, with a greeting from the school, hand their baskets out. We drew up at the first house whose owner's name had been given by the local minister. One of the top class girls and I walked up to the front door and rang the bell. We received no reply, but, undeterred we walked round the side to meet what we were given to understand would be 'a poor old gentleman' The 'poor old gentleman' was cleaning his brand new BMW! He walked jauntily over to us and in appearance, looked about my age. 'And what can I do for you good folks?' he called. My girl offered him the basket of harvest goods and made a pretty speech. He smiled and willingly accepted our gift, but I had the distinct feeling I knew of more deserving old people in the Care Centre in St. Albans.

I believed it was very important for children with such privileged backgrounds to see other children from other schools. I took a party of eleven year olds in the mini bus to visit children at a home run by a friend of mine.

The children enjoying a special visit.

The top class also accompanied old people from the Care Centre in St. Albans to help them do their Christmas shopping. The children ran willingly to fetch possible presents for the old people to examine before purchase. Later the children related their adventures on a tape recorder, which was played on a Parents Evening at the end of the term.

The PTA had a formidable football team. At that time a number of the fathers played for the first and second division teams and there was never any shortage of volunteers from dads who played semi-professionally. A match was arranged by my deputy, against the parents of a school in Hatfield. I am ashamed to admit I know very little about the game but of course I stood on the touchline to cheer on our team. I then became aware of a certain disquiet among our opponents and the Head of the Hatfield school came over to explain his side were 'in for a thrashing'. He pointed out that to begin with we had Bob Wilson in goal and many of our players were professional or played for very well known teams. The game commenced and before half time we were four goals up. It was at that point I suggested we 'lent' the opposition about half our team. The suggestion was gratefully received by the Hatfield parents!

We had a young boy at the school named Simon. He was nationally known for undergoing a bone marrow transplant in the very early days of such operations being performed. One afternoon, I was leaving school quite late when the telephone rang. It was a call from a squadron leader who was enquiring if I had a boy named Simon at my school? I said I had and he wondered if a presentation could be made to Simon by his squadron in recognition of his bravery in undergoing such an operation. I said he could, but I would prefer it if the other children in the school could be involved. This was agreed and a time was set for the visit. I shared this secret only with my wife, who was my secretary and my Deputy Head, asking him to arrange a fire practice on the date arranged at exactly 10 o'clock. The fire alarm sounded and the whole school lined up and were counted on the playground. As this was proceeding, I heard the sound of a helicopter approaching, but still quite high in the sky. A moment later it returned, much lower, followed by three others! I ordered the children to stand perfectly still and to the great surprise of the children and the rest of the staff, four helicopters landed on the school field! I shook hands with the squadron leader who very kindly asked if the children would like to sit in the helicopters as soon as the engines cooled down. While this was happening a group of airmen stood around Simon, who had been given a flying helmet to wear and photographs were taken. Simon was given a huge picture of the squadron signed by all the men. After tea and cakes provided by the kitchen staff, the airmen climbed back into their machines. I asked the squadron leader how far they had flown. 'Oh, only from West Germany' he said and waved goodbye. It was certainly a day to remember.

A brave boy and airmen friends.

I would not wish the reader to assume that Brookmans Park simply lived on 'Headlines events' such as Village Day or the firework evening, as important as they were in cementing the relationship between staff and the parents. It is doubtful whether there were many other primary schools in Hertfordshire who were so well supported by their parents, not only financially, but also in the active interest they took in all the schools activities. We had several parents who were qualified teachers and volunteered their services. I recall one parent who taught drama. In fact this was Bob Wilson's wife, whose three children attended the school. She was always on hand, willing to give her time and experience to the school. Megs was the secretary of the P.T.A for five years and was a wonderful organiser. She supported the drama at the school and I remember particularly on Friday afternoons when, for my wife's sake, I tried to leave at a respectable time, Megs Wilson was always on hand. I once said to her that I was unable to pay her for all her many hours of labour she freely gave to the school. She replied "Please don't talk about money John. It's quite unnecessary". So I said no more.

I remember on one of my school practices thirty years earlier as a trainee teacher, the only time I ever saw the Headmaster was at an assembly once a week. I just could not understand his reasoning. To me, that defeated the whole object of having a Headmaster. One could just as well have an efficient administrator.

Undoubtedly the best day of the week for me was a Wednesday. I took the whole school, infants and juniors, for assembly. I told them stories and we sang old-fashioned hymns. I then presented the Head's cup to any boy or girl who had been noted by the staff for anything that made a difference to the school. For example, particularly good behaviour, tidy uniforms or showing consideration to others. I tended to leave out high academic achievements, since I wanted everyone to feel they had a chance to win. I was delighted when the loudest applause went to a little girl who had learning difficulties, but always gave her best. Her mother told me years later her daughter never forgot the day she won 'Mr Sidnell's cup.' After assembly the infants left as did the junior staff and I continued with all the juniors by myself. We practiced the hymns for later assemblies.

The Best Day of The Week. Wednesday hymn practice, table practice and 'Sirs' story.

This was followed by Table Practice when the top class, who all knew their tables well, gathered together groups of younger children, and with paper and pencils tested them. This was not unlike a recommendation of the Forster Education Act of 1870 where older children taught groups of younger children. They loved it, both the tested and the testers. It was a great honour for the seven year olds to stand on the stage and say their tables to the rest of the school and to be loudly applauded. I promised if they did well, we would finish the session with one of my made up stories. Bribery? – Certainly, but it worked and there were always pleas from the children when the first play bell rang that they didn't mind missing play to hear another story! I used to ask the children where we had reached the previous week and a 'forest of hands' was able to remember to my last sentence! In fairness, I must confess I did receive some mild rebukes from parents who said their children had nightmares on Wednesday nights. After one story had finished and the children were silently filing out of the hall one girl remained. She was eleven and very intelligent. She asked, 'How do you make up stories like that Mr Sidnell?' I explained that I hadn't any idea of what was coming next, so while I was telling the story, I was thinking how it could be developed. She was very impressed and said 'I bet my dad couldn't do that sir'. I smiled and said 'Probably not Katie, but there are so many things your dad could do that would baffle me completely.'

I did impress upon the parents how smart their children looked in their school uniforms. There were no problems here with the girls in their print dresses for the summer term, while the boys always wore shorts, a white shirt, school tie and all the children changed into soft shoes in the school. One parent, whose daughter came from a private school, suggested the girls might like to wear a straw hat in the summer term, but I felt that might be a step too far! The choir, dressed in white blouses and shirts with the school tie, looked particularly smart at the music festivals and I was impressed that the boys had no objection to the girls combing their hair before the school went on stage. I very much doubt whether boys would allow that sort of thing now!

The Inspector Calls.

I recall I had an unexpected visit from an inspector who enquired whether he might walk round the school. I was delighted and asked if I might be excused as I had an important meeting with a parent. I did notice, however, that when he reached the hall door, one of the top class girls stepped forward to open it for him. I met him again at lunch break and his opening remarks were, "Was I aware that my school was twenty years out of date?" He went on to say he saw children of six and seven years of age, 'singing out their tables' and in another class, were copying out lists of spellings to learn as homework.' I did not feel I had to apologise for either of these facts. I did rather daringly say, 'That was the nicest thing I had heard said about my school in a very long time' and pointed out the size of the classes indicated that the parents were not unhappy with my methods. He could not argue with that statement. I recall that same inspector suggested that I should have the entrance hall and junior corridors repainted 'as the existing pale blue made the children 'run'! At first I thought he was joking, but when I saw he was quite serious, I suggested we should watch from my room with the door open, so we could see how many children actually ran without them seeing us. Strangely, he declined the offer!

I wanted to prove to myself that if a subject were approached from a 'fun angle' children would learn things, which seemed impossibly hard. I told them at one of my assemblies I wanted them to surprise their parents with their knowledge. I said I would teach the upper juniors the books of the Bible in their correct order by a 'secret' method. I hasten to add it wasn't that I wanted to 'indoctrinate' the school in any religious beliefs, but for them just learn something hard for the fun of it. There's a simple chorus whose tune can be made to fit the books of the Bible when sung through three times. In no time the children 'cottoned on' and in a matter of weeks we had the books of the Old Testament sorted out, spending less than ten minutes at the end of my assembly. Over the years I have received several e-mails from parents whose children still remember Genesis, Exodus, Leviticus and Numbers, twenty-five years later!

I was reminded by an ex-pupil of something else I taught them 'just for fun'. She is now a parent at the school with three children of her own. She remembered that on one occasion after the Wednesday table practice session I told the children how lucky they were they didn't have to learn their sixteen times table as we did. I went on to explain we had to learn the table as there were sixteen ounces in a pound. I even quoted the table from memory and was immediately faced with the juniors begging to learn it 'just for fun'! They wanted to surprise their teachers at having learned something 'really hard!' Then sometime later at an assembly, I told the staff, that their children had a surprise for them and started them off. The sparkle in their eyes showed just how much they enjoyed 'their' secret, Again, decades later, I have received e-mails from parents who can still remember their sixteen times table!

Readers will understand how teaching can be so much fun and so rewarding. I found there were literally no limits to what a child could achieve, given the right incentives. At Brookmans Park I saw little point in the children standing in a cold playground first thing in the morning when they could be far more use to me.

I asked one particular girl from the top class if she would sit outside my room and read a book for a half an hour before school. If any parent came to see me I asked her to explain that I was engaged with another parent and would they wait? On one occasion I was interviewing a prospective parent and my door was left partly open. I was, of course, listening to the parent who sat before me, but was also half listening to what the top class girl, Kate, was saying outside. The conversation went something like this. Kate: 'Good morning sir. Did you wish to speak with Mr Sidnell, our Headmaster?' A man's voice in the hallway: 'Well, yes I did. Is that possible?' Kate: 'I'm afraid Mr Sidnell has someone with him at the moment'. There was a slight pause and she continued, 'May I be of assistance to you while you are waiting sir?' Again there was a pause and then the voice said 'Well, I don't think you can miss' (I'm not sure Kate would have approved of 'Miss') 'but, I would like to discuss with your Headmaster the possibility of my daughter joining the school.' Kate: "I'm sorry Mr Sidnell is engaged at the moment and clearly it is not within my remit to answer that question, but may I ask the age of your daughter as I'm sure Mr Sidnell would have no objection to me showing you that part of the school.' Their voices faded down the corridor and at this point the parent opposite me paused, as he had obviously heard what Kate had been saying. 'My goodness, Mr Sidnell', he said 'are they all like that?' I agreed that she was very self – confident, but didn't add she was very used to keeping adult company.

I had a request from two mums, asking if they could teach dance to the top classes after school. In my innocence I imagined that the children would be introduced to the waltz and quickstep! The parents asked if the children could wear something more suitable for the lesson. I agreed without thinking of the implications of this request. After school I wandered into the main hall where mostly girls were being introduced to modern dance! Not that they needed much introducing. I was amazed how quickly the girls picked up what I considered most complicated routines. The only equivalent I could imagine was for me to play Bach preludes on the organ. If their ability was a surprise, their dress was quite a shock. It transformed innocent eleven year old girls into what one would expect to see on 'Top of the Pops'.

I was indeed grateful that they agreed to my suggestion to change back into school uniform before leaving the premises. The Chairman of Governors, a great friend of mine, once asked me a question at a P.T.A dance. "How do you play the piano so well, but find extreme difficulty in dancing the Waltz or Quick Step"? I had no answer to that question!

They say a filament in an electric light bulb glows brighter before it burns out. In a strange way this was happening to me. I was nearing my first ten years at the school and my mind was filled with new ideas I wanted to try out to extend the scope for the children's work. I was usually at my desk soon after 7.30 in the morning, preparing my story for assembly, which the children loved. I would snatch a fifteen-minute break at lunchtime, although my door was always open for the staff to see me. I then managed to fit recorders in sometime in the lunch period as I required some of the children for choir after school.

CHAPTER 26

The Great Shock for the Headmaster
– Brookmans Park School

For no reason I could imagine, I caught a cough. This was unheard of as far as I was concerned. I always enjoyed excellent health. It was persistent and I was forced to see a doctor. Worse was to follow. He announced I had 'whooping cough' and I was confined to bed for three weeks. When I returned I still felt weak and unsure of myself. My doctor suggested I should consult the Medical Officer of Health as a matter of common sense. This I did and after a lengthy examination he smiled and said 'Tell me Mr Sidnell, what is the first date you can retire?' I was dumb founded! I could hardly believe what I was hearing! In a shaky voice I enquired what the problem was? 'You have a heart murmur and show every sign of exhaustion. You'll need months of rest.' When I told my wife, her first thought was how we should tell the staff, parents and children at the school. They had been my life for the last decade. I was only fifty-five and still felt I could continue for at least five years. I even suggested to the Education Officer that if I worked at a slower pace, I might continue. He would have none of it saying 'No, Mr Sidnell, we are not at County Hall having our Heads fall down on the job. You have served the county excellently for almost forty years and its time to stop.'

Towards the end of term I called in my deputy to tell

him the sad news. We had worked together so well for ten years. Needless to say he was shocked and immediately offered to take my place next term. Alas, the county did not agree. I called the whole staff together and announced my retirement at the end of the summer term. I felt very emotional having made the announcement and retired to my room. I knew village news travelled fast and before the end of the afternoon I had many parents coming in to see me, shaking their heads in disbelief and asking what they should say to their children who would be devastated by the news. I remember a girl knocked on my door at the end of school that day. She was crying and through her tears she said she was so sad, 'But only one thing cheers me up sir!' I asked her what that could possibly be. 'I'm also leaving this term. I couldn't have come back next term without you sir.' I thought her sentiments were most touching.

From that moment onwards I looked at school in a most nostalgic way. I attended the last governors meeting, the last P.T.A meeting and finally the last week in my teaching career.

The deputy came to see me with a request. Could I possibly take the last Thursday off? I somewhat reluctantly agreed, mentally making a note that I should have to be in before 7.00 on the last day. He explained rather vaguely that the parents wanted to give me 'a good send off and would Doreen and I return at 7pm on the Thursday evening?' I had absolutely no idea what was in store for us, until, on driving through the village that evening I noticed the flags and bunting decked over trees and hedges all the way along the road to school! The school itself was decked overall. It looked like the trooping of the colours! We went into the main hall and were greeted by over five hundred parents and ex pupils.

The canteen next door was just as full. What happened in the next two hours will stay in my memory forever. The Divisional Officer had been invited and said lots of nice things about me including something about my academic record from college, which I would have preferred he hadn't. I always regarded my interest in the teaching of children as more of a knack than due to any high academic achievement. The gifts I received seem to continue through the evening. Apart from the gifts of silverware, engraved plates and goblets, Doreen and I had chosen a magnificent overstrung piano and stool with the money donated by the parents and children. The stage curtains were opened to gasps of surprise from all the parents and ex pupils present. I suppose I should have played some great march. I know the parents would have enjoyed that, but frankly, I was too overcome by the great and genuine kindness everyone had shown Doreen and I. Eventually I managed to thank everyone, not just for the wonderful presents, but perhaps even more importantly, for their great friendship over ten happy years I had the privilege of being their Headmaster. We drank champagne with every sort of delicacy from the tables. I know on the way home that night, Doreen said little. I glanced across the car at her and tears were streaming down her face. In a very real way it was our school, not mine!

In a sense the last day was almost an anticlimax. I took my last assembly. I changed the board, which indicated the special words for the week from 'A Good Finish' to 'Our School'

Our School. The Final Curtain.

I was so very proud of the children and staff who had made it all possible. The children sang their last hymn beautifully and in my prayer I asked God to bless each one of them. I returned to my room and filled in my logbook for the last time and then my wife and I walked onto the field together, for only I knew just what she had contributed to the smooth running of the administration of the school. I honestly wasn't interested in that part of school administration and the fact she loved every minute of it, meant we complimented each other perfectly. I was quite convinced that Doreen would be as greatly missed by the mums, as I would be by the children.

As I recall on the day that the auditors came to the school each year, they would enquire before they commenced if 'My good lady' was still 'cooking the books'. I smiled and confirmed she was and Mr Clark said 'Excellent! Your wife is never a penny out. We shall finish early today.' Her office next to mine was so often filled with laughter as Doreen and the mothers shared some private joke. As if to prove my point on the last afternoon, she was presented with forty-one huge bouquets of flowers.

She received so many one of the fathers volunteered to take them home in his estate car. The children lined the drive from the school and waved and cheered for the last time. We waved and smiled through tears.

Goodbye for the last time.

CHAPTER 27

Something Completely Different.

I was very unwell following my retirement. I had been working with great enthusiasm and enjoyment for ten years at Brookmans Park School and I had truly given it my all. I saw a specialist who counselled complete rest for a year. I lay on the sofa listening to classical music and also catching up with the reading I had neglected for years, but my mind constantly returned to my school, wondering how the deputy was finding his 'new job'? He was acting Head until the new Headmaster commenced after Christmas. I had no qualms as to his competence, but working as a Head with a staff he already knew well can have its problems! I found it very hard to convince myself that wasn't my problem anymore.

As the months passed I began to feel better. My wife and I had been keen to caravan and we started to take short breaks to sites in England. Doreen always enjoyed such holidays and when I suggested we should spread our wings and take holidays abroad, she became enthusiastic. We visited friends in South Africa on numerous occasions and when my parents died, we felt we could begin our holidays on a grand scale.

Doreen lived for animals. We owned a Labrador and for a decade when I was Head at Brookmans Park, he sat under my wife's desk and was taken out several times a day by pairs of children for exercise. I know my wife would have wished me to add one tale concerning our dog Sandy. He was adored by the children and especially by the children whose parents didn't own dogs. An amusing incident occurred once when the school hall was filled with parents preparing for a Jumble Sale on the Friday night. Sandy was sitting outside my room, watching all the activity and receiving the occasional pat from parents as they passed into the hall. Suddenly he stood up and almost ran into the hall. Something he had never done before. He stopped opposite a particular mother and begged! I went into the hall to see what all the fuss was about. I saw this mother with her hand over her mouth in surprise. She rather shame-faced admitted that when her daughter took Sandy for a walk, she used to call in her home so that Sandy could beg for a biscuit! He recognised her voice over all the others in the hall!

Our South African holidays ranged from visits to Durban to Cape Town, and from Johannesburg to Kruger Park. We borrowed our friends Mercedes Benz and drove up to Zimbabwe to view the Victoria Falls, a never to be forgotten sight. With my health improving we flew to places as distant as Borneo for Doreen to hold hands with the Orang-utans. We visited Singapore and Hong Kong. We watched the sun go down over the Maldives and explored the smallest islands of the West Indies, all in the space of ten years. The world was our oyster.

Then suddenly everything changed. We were on a cruise from Durban to Naples and on a particular afternoon we were in the ships lift returning to our cabin, when Doreen, for no reason, suddenly left the lift a floor too early. I ran down the stairs to find her wandering and staring about her in a dazed manner. She was unable to account for her behaviour, but in the following days it became obvious something was terribly wrong. Once back in England, we saw a specialist who confirmed my worst fears. She had Alzheimer's and had probably had it for the best part of two years. Sadly, there is no cure and for the following five years I watched my vivacious wife who had single handedly ran the administration for a school of over three hundred children and staff with great efficiency and kindness, turn into a shadow of her former self. She lost touch with reality and the friends she made throughout her life. Finally, I had to let her go into an excellent care home where she spent the final three years of her life. Naturally I visited her several times a week but in her last months she recognised just me. When I visited her she smiled, but alas, she could no longer speak. Days later she was transferred to hospital and died without regaining consciousness. We first met when I waved to her in the playground at Beaumont School. We had been blissfully married for fifty-two years.

I believed I was then to spend the rest of my life with wonderful memories of education, but suddenly my brother and I had a request to speak to the 16 year olds at Beaumont School which we attended at the beginning of the war, as part of the GCSE course in history. We were delighted to accept the invitation and for the last five years we have talked to a hundred pupils at a time on Wartime Britain. We found the pupils delightful and the question time that followed proved their genuine interest in the subject. Our talks were followed by literally hundreds of letters of appreciation with yet more questions. Personally, I was delighted with their interest in wartime music and was very happy to play a selection of my wartime favourites including the great Glen Miller. Last year we extended our talks to include a session with the eighteen year olds and their teachers.

We must make a final observation about the student's fascination with what was allowed as punishment for children over sixty years ago. We all agreed that if teachers today used the cane as they did then, they would be imprisoned. We met one of our masters long after he had retired. As my brother and I were together, he recognised us and sneered "I know you chaps. You're the Sidnell twins. Now let me guess what you do for a living? Did you become road sweepers or was it dustbin men"? I smiled and was able to tell him that we both became Headmasters. He couldn't believe it! Personally, we were delighted to see that education had moved on and the schools today are blessed with such enlightened teachers.

There are many jobs that pay more than I ever received, but I venture to suggest there are very few that would give that wonderful sense of satisfaction we felt in taking part in forming the lives of future citizens.

A further selection of school photographs

A parent tells the class about her work.

Easter bonnet competitions

History and Handwork combined 3rd year.

A quiet time by the pond at lunch break.

Reception class cooks for Mr Sidnell.

What dad does for a living- Talks by the children.

Fun with apple bobbing.

The third year remember the war.

Christmas dinner served by the staff.

Parents invited to an assembly.

Miniature gardens competition.

The Staff 1974.